What Mean?

~

Where Russians Go Wrong
in English

What Mean?

~

Where Russians Go Wrong in English

Lynn Visson

HIPPOCRENE BOOKS, INC.
New York

For information, address:
HIPPOCRENE BOOKS, INC.
171 Madison Ave.
New York, NY 10016

www.hippocrenebooks.com

Library of Congress Cataloging-in-Publication Data

Visson, Lynn.
 What mean? : where Russians go wrong in English / Lynn Visson.
    pages cm.
 ISBN 978-0-7818-1322-8 (pbk.) -- ISBN 0-7818-1322-0 (pbk.)
 1. English language--Study and teaching--Russian speakers. 2. English
language--Spoken English. 3. English language--Social aspects.
4. Language and culture. I. Title.
 PE1129.S4V54 2013
 428.2'49171--dc23
                                        2013026770

Printed in the United States of America.

Contents

Preface   vii

CHAPTER 1. Introduction: Language and Culture   1

CHAPTER 2. Think Positive   11

CHAPTER 3. Think Negative   25

CHAPTER 4. Think Active or Passive?   45

CHAPTER 5. Etiquette and Behavior   57

CHAPTER 6. The Time Is Out of Joint   89

CHAPTER 7. The Art of Eating   99

CHAPTER 8. English — A Linguistic Headache   111

CHAPTER 9. Nonverbal Language   133

Endnotes   145

Preface

〜

"What mean?" The problems faced by English-speaking Russians have been part of my life as long as I can remember. Though both my Russian émigré parents spoke English very well, their pet errors were ingrained in their speech for life. Born in St. Petersburg, my mother spoke four languages fluently, and her English was remarkably free from most of the common grammatical errors made by Russians. Yet to the end of her 97 years she would come out with "What mean?" as a rendering of «Что значит?» followed by the word or expression she needed: "What mean, 'expatiate'?" My equally quadrilingual and highly educated father was from Kiev, and his excellent English was also frequently studded with such "Russianisms" as "the soul hurts" or "not possible."

Russian English remained in my life well after I left my parents' home. For 35 years I spoke Russian at home with my Muscovite husband, Boris Rabbot, whose literary, flawless Russian never failed to astound our émigré friends. Although he never went back to his native country after he emigrated in 1976, Boris preserved the purity of his native language until his death in 2011. His great sensitivity, refined politeness, and courtesy, however, were frequently not in evidence when he had to express himself in English. "No, it is not allowed" or "It is not necessary to do this" sounded jarring to his American counterparts. And he was no exception. Over and over I have heard highly educated and sensitive Russian émigrés sound abrasive or rude, affected or snobbish, when they were in fact anything but that. The reverse is also true, for due to their linguistic and cultural gaps many of my American academic colleagues and students, to their dismay, unwittingly have offended the feelings of Soviet acquaintances with utterances that savaged the Russian language.

That is what inspired me to write this book. During my ten years of teaching Russian in American universities, decades of working with Russians in the U.S. and with Americans in Russia, and twenty-five years as a simultaneous interpreter at the United Nations, I became increasingly concerned by such linguistic-cultural misunderstandings. Speakers tended to assume that many expressions and idioms in their native language would work in literal translation, occasionally with disastrous results. Americans speaking Russian in the USSR during both the Soviet and the post-perestroika period frequently wound up in awkward situations, and the same held true for Russian visitors, delegates, tourists, or émigrés speaking English in the U.S.

It is my hope that this book will help students of Russian and English, teachers, translators, interpreters, businesspeople, tourists, émigrés, and all those who daily find themselves obliged to use both Russian and English, avoid such errors. These kinds of linguistic-cultural flubs are also highly disruptive to the spouses in Russian-American marriages, as I often saw while interviewing couples for *Wedded Strangers: The Challenges of Russian-American Marriages* (New York: Hippocrene Books, 2001).

I consulted with Boris on almost every example in this book, checking with him on the original forms of the expressions distorted by Russian native speakers when speaking English. Like so many of my other books, this is a joint one. It is to his memory that this book is dedicated.

1

Introduction:
Language and Culture
∼

Language has a setting ... language does not exist
apart from culture.[1]

Why does an educated and sophisticated visiting Russian professor often sound strange or rude when speaking English to his American friends? And why does an American businessman attempting to cultivate good relationships with his Russian colleagues sound aggressive or dismissive when speaking their language? All too frequently, the causes of miscommunication between speakers of various languages are not phonetic, lexical, grammatical, or syntactic mistakes, but rather a failure to understand the culture in which the language is embedded.[2]

Does a native Russian speaker see the world the same way as an American native speaker of English? Does *"Right away!"* mean the same thing as «сейчас», and is *"Come over for a cup of tea"* the equivalent of «Заходите на чашку чая»? In the U.S. "right away" usually means "within the next few minutes," while for a Russian this may indicate a period ranging from "in five minutes" to "within half an hour." For a Russian that "cup of tea" means a hot drink accompanied by a wide variety of cakes, cookies, and various snacks, while for an American the phrase means just that—a cup of tea, with, perhaps, a lonely cookie for company.

Our languages are vital to forming our cultures and yet are also their products. Dozens of hotly debated theories and heavy tomes have supported or contested these assertions, for the simple question, "What is culture?" has been the subject of endless argument among linguists, anthropologists, and historians. Since there is universal agreement that culture is passed on from one person to another and is accepted by a group, it cannot and does not exist in a vacuum.[3] The idea that language and culture are interdependent and determine and impact one another is not, however, universally accepted.[4] Today, the theory that language is a product of a specific culture, rather than a universal alphabet of semantic concepts pre-imprinted on the mind, is known as the Sapir-Whorf hypothesis.[5] Named after the German-born American anthropologist and linguist Edward Sapir (1884-1939), and the American linguist Benjamin Lee Whorf (1897-1941), this theory posits that language is a decisive factor in forming our views of the world because it provides speakers with a set of elements, including grammar, that predispose them to perceive their environment in certain patterns.

For Whorf the structure of a language, which is a product of a speaker's culture, is decisive for his mentality. "Language ... is not merely a reproducing instrument for voicing ideas but rather is itself the shaper of ideas," he wrote, "the program and guide for the individual's mental activity, for his analysis of impressions ..."[6] Sapir agreed that perception of the world is determined by language, in turn the product of the speaker's culture. Grammar and vocabulary, which vary from language to language, impact the patterns of thought and perception on which we build our concepts of reality.

In any language, many of the words used to describe the life and phenomena of a country or culture have no precise equivalents in other tongues. Convinced that language could only be understood within a cultural context, Sapir posited that, "no two languages are ever sufficiently similar to be considered as representing the same reality. The worlds in which different societies live are distinct worlds, not merely the same world with different labels."[7]

The Sapir-Whorf hypothesis is diametrically opposed to the well-known American linguist Noam Chomsky's theory that language is "innate and preprogrammed," generated in each individual by universal principles. "Human beings," Sapir asserted, "are very much at the mercy of the particular language which has become the medium of expression for their society ..."[8] Vocabulary, Sapir emphasized, is highly dependent on culture. "It goes without saying," he wrote, "that the mere content of language is intimately related to culture. A society that has no knowledge of theosophy need have no name for it; aborigines that had never seen or heard of a horse were compelled to invent or borrow a word for the animal when they made its acquaintance."[9] He explicitly linked the development of language content to culture: "Vocabulary is a very sensitive index of the culture of a people and changes of the meaning, loss of old words, the creation and borrowing of new ones are all dependent on the history of culture itself."[10]

Living in today's global village, and acquiring increasing linguistic and cultural sophistication, many people are acutely aware of the differences between their own and foreign linguistic-cultural environments. What does an individual then do? Does he try to adapt to a new language and culture, or does he retreat into linguistic-cultural isolationism? Or does he attempt to force his knowledge and perception of his own language into the Procrustean bed of another tongue, forever speaking "Russianized English" or "Anglicized Russian"? An option that leads straight down the road to linguistic and cultural misunderstanding.

A sophisticated language speaker, however, may be well aware of the real differences existing between the world-views of various languages and deliberately adapt to them when switching from one tongue to another. This book is attempting to convey this kind of heightened awareness of such differences between Russian and English.

The eminent Russian linguist V. N. Komissarov emphasized that similar words and expressions seem very different to various individuals because of the distinctions imposed by their languages.[11] For example, the word «дом» does not conjure up the same image for Russian and English speakers. In English the word can mean either "*house*" (a physical unit, edifice, dwelling, or building serving as living quarters) or "*home*" (a place of residence, as well as the social unit formed by a family living together).[12] In Russian, however, the emphasis is on "home," not on a "house" in the sense of a building.

It has been argued that only proper names, geographic, scientific, and technical terms, days of the week, months, and numerals have full lexical correspondence—i.e., mean exactly the same things to everyone, regardless of language. But «воскресенье» in Russian refers to the resurrection of Christ, while the etymology of the word "Sunday" in English is associated with the sun.

Though «два» and *two* are absolute equivalents, a "*two-bedroom apartment*" means different things in Russian and English. In America a "two-bedroom apartment" in fact has three or more rooms, including a living room, a kitchen, and perhaps a terrace, while in Russia а «двухкомнатная квартира» means exactly what it says—an apartment consisting of two rooms, usually a living room and one bedroom along with a kitchen and a bathroom, but not an apartment with two bedrooms.[13]

The American anthropologist Edward Hall commented that, "no two languages are alike ... Some are so dissimilar ... that they force the speaker into two different versions of reality."[14] The nature of a language and its speakers' shared assumptions mold their views of both their own group's culture and of the outside world.

Vital to understanding linguistic and cultural differences are the "key words"[15] of a given language and culture. What words, concepts, and values does a society favor? Which does it disdain or discard? Try to find accurate English translations for «тоска», «душа», or «духовность», or Russian equivalents for the English words "privacy," "equality," and "committed."[16] The Russian word «тоска» in the expression «тоска по родине» can be rendered in English as "homesickness," and «она тоскует по маме» as "She misses her mother." In other contexts, however, «тоска» may point to "yearning," "longing," or "anguish." This blend of nostalgia, yearning, longing, anguish, misery, melancholy, depression, or boredom incarnates a complex of gloomy sentiments with which a good many "positive-thinking" Americans do not easily identify.

In the U.S. an entire book has been written on the elusive, incomprehensible concept—a key one for Russian culture—of the Russian soul, «душа», a word that pops up in dozens of Russian idioms.[17] If translated literally, these Russian expressions with "soul" will sound quite odd and only reinforce the American stereotype of Russians as irrational, Dostoevskian characters. In English, equivalent expressions for the word "soul" are often replaced by "heart" (heartfelt sympathy / from the bottom of my heart):

Со всей душой, от души   *With all my heart*
В глубине души чувствую … *In my heart (I feel that …)*
Душа нараспашку *To wear one's heart on one's sleeve*

In talking about people, Americans tend to emphasize "intelligence" and "mind" more than "heart" or "soul." The common Russian notion of a «задушевная беседа» (*heart-to-heart talk*) can seem strange to Americans who live in a culture that prefers restraint and moderation in relationships.[18]

Many common English and Russian words and innocent-looking phrases would seem to have exact equivalents in translation. But "He is my friend" and «Он—мой друг» in fact mean very different things in Russia and the U.S., for, as we will see in this book, the assumptions underlying the Russian and English words for "friend" and "friendship" are worlds apart.

Does the Russian expression «она поправилась» mean something good or bad? The idea is that "she's looking better" (the root of the word is the positive notion «прав»). But, since this also means "she's put on weight," is it a bad thing (which is nearly always the case in America)? Asking at length about someone's health may be welcomed in one culture and avoided in another. What on earth does «он сухой человек» (literally, "He's a dry person") mean to an American? That someone looks like a dried-out prune? How do we know if «рука» is a hand or an arm? And are «пальцы» fingers or toes?

The goal of translation and interpretation is to find the correct language "keys" to transcend linguistic and cultural barriers. The Russian expert on translation A. D. Shveitser wrote that, "Translation means not only the interaction of languages, but the interaction of cultures. The process of translation crosses both linguistic and cultural borders."[19] As people with different languages and cultures interact on a daily basis, there is an ever-greater need to understand these distinctions.

Lexical items do not exist in a cultural vacuum, and it is often hard for a non-native speaker to realize which key words critical to the understanding of a culture have quite different associations within another language and culture. While for a U.S. citizen "America" may be associated with "patriotism" and "love," for an Al Qaeda terrorist it symbolizes "the evil power."

Each culture may also show significant linguistic variations among native speakers, depending on geographical location (urban vs. rural, north vs. south), age, education, ethnic origin, profession, etc. A New Yorker of Polish Jewish origin does not speak the same English as a black shopkeeper in small-town Mississippi, just as a graying Moscow University professor does not speak the same Russian as a young sailor from Murmansk.

Situations, role, and context also strongly impact the language of native speakers. A Russian may have difficulty distinguishing the differences in how his American boss, a waiter, or a friend address him. Forgetting where and from whom he has heard a specific phrase, the Russian may end up addressing a business colleague with words he has heard an American friend use when talking to a gas-station attendant. Trying to sound "native" is an extremely dangerous undertaking. To "blend in" and show off mastery of the language and milieu, a non-native speaker often tries to sound as colloquial as possible. Yet a Russian who insists on saying "I'm gonna" and "I wanna," or who sprinkles his conversation with "Wazzup?"[20] because he has heard these terms used by native speakers of English, will not sound "native." Instead he will come across as uneducated or simply boorish. Though these incorrect forms are common currency on the street, in buses, bars, and restaurants, their use will only convince the American listener that his foreign interlocutor is not very literate.

At the opposite extreme, in the past many Russians spoke excessively formal "Moscow English," coming across as condescending, patronizing, or as though they had just stepped out of another century. So too, countless Americans have made very strange impressions on Russians by trying to speak just "as they do," referring to everything as «клево» (*cool*), or, far worse, using «матерные слова» (*four-letter words*) picked up from a Russian friend over a couple of drinks.

Since the U.S. is home to so many immigrants and foreigners,

Americans tend to be rather tolerant of pronunciation and grammar errors, which ordinarily evoke a polite correction or a friendly smile. They are far less indulgent, however, of mistakes caused by ignorance of the culture. A Russian asking, "Did he earn very much money?" is not merely misusing modifiers indicating quantity. The negative reaction from his American interlocutor results from cultural and not linguistic factors. "Why is he asking about how much that man earned?" "It's none of his business!" is the American's reaction. Questions such as, "Did he do all right for himself?"/ "Did he manage?"/ "Did he come out all right?" or simply, "Did he do well?" would be a much more acceptable way of inquiring whether the individual was financially successful. Because direct questions concerning how much someone earns are not customary in the U.S., the behavioral error is compounding a grammatical one.

A native speaker may well attribute a foreigner's inappropriate use of language to personal behavioral characteristics rather than to linguistic ignorance. A request such as "Bring me soup!" is more likely to make an American think "Boy, is he rude!" than that the Russian has not learned how to politely make a request to a waiter. Failure to grasp the unwritten rules of the language-culture duo can make an educated Russian sound like a boor in English, and the same holds true for many a well-brought-up American.

An excellent knowledge of a language does not necessarily entail in-depth knowledge of the culture. A Russian's ability to speak fluent and colloquial "American" English does not mean that he likes or accepts American culture, or that he genuinely understands how Americans feel about their country. As the journalist Ian Buruma commented in regard to foreigners, monolingual and monocultural Americans tend to assume that, "just because they speak English, eat McDonald's hamburgers and watch Hollywood films, they must be just like Americans."[21] Likewise, Americans speaking "very good" Russian may be light years away from a true understanding of Russian culture.

True, there have always been talented individuals who achieve near-native mastery of a language. It is indeed ironic that the foreigner with a very good knowledge of English may be in greater danger of committing certain kinds of errors than someone with limited mastery of the language. "Sometimes we are confused, puzzled, or even angry when a foreigner's speech is too close to our own because it makes it harder to remember that he may not share our beliefs and attitudes …. A 'foreign accent' may have its uses," commented the British sociolinguist Ronald Macaulay.[22] It is all too easy to assume that familiarity with a language also means familiarity with the culture in which that language is embedded. The better the knowledge of a language, the more striking the ignorance of its culture. As one Russian observer rightly commented, «чем лучше говорит на каком-то языке человек, тем более странным выглядит его несогласующееся с этим языком поведение».[23]

An in-depth understanding of a language and culture requires a grasp of both its rapidly changing key concepts and new phenomena. There is a wide gap between the difficulty in translating concrete country-specific phenomena—i.e. «вид на жительство», «ЗАГС», a "Metrocard," "golden parachute" or "country fair"—and in coming up with the meaning of abstract, culturally defined concepts with no direct equivalent in another language, such as «умиление» and «тоска» or "privacy" and "sophistication."

Many English words and concepts have found their way into post-perestroika Russian, and cognates such as «имидж», «пиар» and «хеджирование» have now acquired their own identity in the language. Not every cognate or borrowing, however, retains its original meaning. For example, the meaning of the English word "killer" is not identical to that of the Russian borrowing «киллер». In English the word "killer" can refer to any kind of murderer, while the Russian word «киллер» specifically refers to a «наемный убийца» (*hit man* or *contract killer*).[24] And the English borrowing "babushka" is not a translation of the Russian word for "grandmother," but refers to a scarf worn over the head and tied under the chin.

One author has suggested that all the terms and concepts allegedly so "unique" to a language that they cannot be rendered properly in any other tongue be compiled into a "Dictionary of Untranslatables."[25] In the minds of native speakers numerous specific cultural associations are linked to such "untranslatable" —and sometimes even with easily translatable—words, and great care must be taken when rendering these into another language. These lacunae in translation do not exist solely on the linguistic level. Gestures, body language, pauses, and silence as well as verbal utterances are part of a single linguistic-cultural "package" of behavior formed by and reflecting cultural values.

It is the task of the translator, the interpreter, the cultural mediator, and others working in the field of cross-cultural communication to try to find explanations and equivalents for «реалии» (*translatables*) and untranslatables that work in terms of both language and culture. One American corporate executive rightly commented, "it was easy to master a foreign language; it's the culture that trips you up."

As an American of Russian background, a teacher of Russian language and literature, simultaneous interpreter and translator, author of a book on Russian-American marriages and works on translation, interpretation, and various aspects of Russian language and culture, I have spent years encountering and observing these problems of cultural miscommunication. This book is a modest contribution to help in finding a solution to some of these linguistic and cultural misunderstandings.

2

Think Positive
~

Americans are raised to believe in *The Power of Positive Thinking*, the title of the classic bestseller by the well-known Protestant minister Norman Vincent Peale (1898-1994).[26] "Positive thinking" means possessing a relentlessly positive attitude towards life and other people, the belief that, though there may be setbacks, in the long run things will "work out." Dr. Peale's "power of positive thinking" became as American as apple pie. It is a *sine qua non* for success and happiness in all areas of life, in relating to family and friends, at work and at play. Both in Hollywood movies and daily life the words "Everything is going to be all right" have been uttered (with heartfelt sincerity) in thousands of difficult or tragic situations. The book was a logical outcome of Dale Carnegie's 1936 classic, *How to Win Friends and Influence People,* in which "positive thinking" comes perilously close to the risky delusion that the mind's positive force can impact the surrounding world, change negatives to positives, "make everything all right."[27]

Basically, for Americans everything is "fine" or "great." If you've made a date to see someone, he will say, "Great, see you Tuesday." And when you're saying good-bye to him after having seen him on Tuesday? "It was great to see you." To a Russian such hyperbole as "How was the movie?" "Super/great/marvelous/terrific" or "Why don't you come over for dinner on Tuesday?" "Thanks, that would be fantastic" unless spoken between two teenagers would sound mildly hysterical and completely inappropriate. «Отлично / хорошо / с удовольствием» would be normal responses to such an invitation.

The longstanding tradition of thinking positive, of showing a positive face to the world regardless of how one is really feeling, has had an enormous impact on American language and behavior. Such positive thinking is not, as it may often seem to foreigners, the result of the kind of absolute naiveté expressed by Voltaire's Candide, convinced despite a rain of disasters and misfortunes, that "everything is for the best in the best of all possible worlds." It is perfectly obvious that thousands of Americans and Russians do not lead an easy, carefree life. This kind of positive thinking, however, is intrinsically alien to the Russian mentality, which prefers to expect the worst and be pleasantly surprised if things turn out more positively.

Americans believe that holding to this optimistic point of view actually makes them feel better. In America no one wants to deal with a negatively minded individual, a whiner or a "loser." The underlying philosophy for millions of Americans (though more often than not they are quite unaware of this) is the Protestant work ethic based on the theories of the German economist Max Weber. Gloomy Calvinism, with its pessimistic theories of predestination, is answered by the premise that good work will be rewarded, both here and in the next life. Economic crises notwithstanding, honest work is the only—and surefire—way to success, financial and social. A problem is not a reason for despair; it is a challenge to be met head-on and overcome.

Scarlett O'Hara's line from the book/movie *Gone with the Wind*, "Tomorrow is another day," neatly sums up the idea that there is always the possibility for improving a situation, for finding a solution, no matter how bleak the circumstances. One Russian translation of Margaret Mitchell's book blithely ignores the implicit idea that there is always hope, rendering "Tomorrow is another day" (which could well be translated as «Утро вечера мудренее») as «Новый день—другие заботы» (*A new day, new cares.*)

For the American, everything in life depends on the individual, who must shoulder full responsibility for his words and actions and "go for the gold," i.e. the gold medal the athlete is striving to win. Blaming others or one's surroundings for various misfortunes wins no sympathy. Throwing up one's hands and saying with a deep sigh, «А что я могу делать?» (*So what can I do about that?*) is not the "American way."

American bookstores are bursting with best-selling volumes by people who have overcome all kinds of adversity—wars, imprisonment, torture, racial discrimination, abject poverty, starvation, floods, alpine disasters, sports accidents, breast cancer, polio, schizophrenia, depression, incest, rape, spousal abuse, alcoholism, and drug addiction, let alone lost elections or public disgrace. The excesses of this kind of superpositive attitude have been brilliantly analyzed and demolished by Barbara Ehrenreich, who in her book, *Bright-Sided: How the Relentless Promotion of Positive Thinking Has Undermined America*, demonstrates how such "blind positive thinking" can numb people to the crisis situation around them and to rational attempts to overcome problems.[28] This culture, she argued, is dangerous, for relentlessly optimistic forecasts regarding sub-prime mortgages and the illusion of increasing real estate values spawned by this positive thinking are signposts on the road to economic and financial disaster.[29]

The positive-thinking individuals who have overcome adversity are "heroes" to Americans or, to use the politically correct term, "survivors," for such individuals are never referred to as "victims." The American must develop a positive image of himself and boldly present that image to the outside world. In a country of individualists one does not hesitate to praise the "positive self" and to show a "positive face" to the outside world, to "pat oneself on the back." There is always "another day," "it will all somehow work out." You only have to "believe in yourself." Despite a severe economic crisis and massive unemployment, positive thinking is still an integral part of the American psyche.

From a very young age, Americans are lectured in school about the importance of good posture, and of standing up straight. Looking healthy and energetic, shoulders forward, facing the surrounding world—all this is part of the "positive" look.

This is particularly important at job interviews, where the American notion is that you not only have to "think positively about yourself" but also to present yourself in a positive light. Despite the collapse of the Soviet regime and the transformative impact of Western capitalism, the notion of "tooting your own horn" (хвалить самого себя) is still somewhat foreign to the Russian mentality. Self-praise and touting one's good qualities smacks of boasting, as shown by the old Russian saying, a play on words popular during the Soviet decades, «Я последняя буква алфавита» («Я» means "I" in Russian and is also the last letter of the alphabet, i.e., "I am the last letter of the alphabet.") More than one Russian has failed to obtain a position in the U.S. due to excessive modesty during a job interview, or as a result of going to the opposite extreme out of nervousness and the knowledge that some kind of self-praise is needed. In the U.S., an individual who does not stress his positive self-image and engage in aggressive self-presentation will come across as bland, passive, and basically uninterested in the job.

The positive thinking that pervades every aspect of American life is continually fueled by a consumer culture. An unhappy client will not make purchases or buy or rent a house; an unhappy worker will not go the extra mile for his employer. One goal of advertising is to make undesirable and useless products look desirable and useful. The resulting hyperbole has contaminated all aspects of American life. A person who has managed to recover from a near-fatal illness has had a "life-affirming experience." No one is "fired;" there is "downsizing." Being shown the door after an interview reveals a "failure to achieve mutual understanding."

The differences between the Russian and American mentalities are visible even in the "positive reflexes" inculcated in children starting on the playground. Where a Russian mother will warn her child against possible dangers—«Смотри, не падай» (*Watch out, don't fall*) or «Осторожно, не пачкайся» (*Careful, don't get yourself dirty*)—many American mothers will send the toddler off with "Have fun! You can do it!"

A great deal has been said and written on both sides of the ocean regarding the perpetual American smile and the impression generally non-smiling Russians make on Americans. An American is told by his family, friends, neighbors, and colleagues to "keep smiling" (что бы ни было, улыбайся, держи улыбку). That grin is learned in childhood, a virtually automatic reflex response to the surrounding world, signaling pleasure at making a new acquaintance, common courtesy, and a readiness to engage in social conversation. The Russian saying, «Смех без причины—признак дурачины» does not hold true for Americans, who do not feel that a smile on meeting a stranger may point to a lack of «серьезность», that a person who is smiling with no apparent cause is a "clown" (как клоун), or that a "hypocritical smile" may only be designed to cover up the speaker's hidden agenda.[30] For Russians a smile must have a reason behind it—and this must be an *emotional* reason. While in the U.S. a smile fulfills a social and not an emotional function, for a Russian it must express feelings: sincere warmth, trust, liking, friendship, and more rarely, gratitude. The smile is not a part of etiquette, but of emotional life.[31] If a Russian is feeling out of sorts, he will definitely not be smiling—he will be seeking sympathy for his unhappy state: «он хочет, чтобы о его беде знал весь мир; ну, если уж не весь мир, пусть хоть весь микрорайон.»[32]

Americans sometimes misinterpret the scowling Russian face on the street as a hostile one. In Russia, however, the non-smile is the standard expression as opposed to the American smile, inculcated from early childhood as part and parcel of "think positive."

One Russian observer has pointed to the striking differences between American positive thinking and the non-smiling, highly critical attitude of many of his fellow-countrymen: «Желание все критиковать, поругать знакомо каждому русскому. Отсюда и хмурость, неулыбчивость, невеселость характера и выражения лица».[33] This radical distinction in attitude has great importance for communication and linguistic behavior. Americans generally expect things to go well and become upset when they do not, while Russians, particularly of the older generation, tend to be far more pessimistic, expect things to go badly, and are pleasantly surprised when this is not the case.

Today, in many large Russian hotels and elegant stores, foreign-trained Russian personnel who have been told to "keep smiling" strain their mouths into such a perpetually twisted grin that even Americans are mildly amused. Or the Russian may flash a mask-like grimace that switches off in a flash, leaving behind a grim and stony face. For Americans, the transition from a smile to a normal expression involves a gradual return of the face to its usual look.

Though ingrained optimism and a positive, benevolent attitude towards others are distinctive features of the American national character, being constantly told to "Come on, smile!" can be rather annoying. A response such as "I'm really a bit out of sorts today" or "I'm really a bit under the weather" is a polite solution.

The American attitude is also voiced in the clichéd idioms accompanying the ubiquitous smile, such as the widespread "Have a nice day." to which Americans pay no more attention than they do to the ads urging them to "Drink Coca-Cola." "Have a nice day" is the expression of a wish or hope, i.e., "I *hope* you have a nice day," and not a command or order to do so, as Russians sometimes interpret it. This hackneyed phrase has become an ongoing irritant to many people, particularly those who are definitely not having a nice day or know that they are not going to have one. I will never forget how the hospital nurse who phoned to tell me that my mother had died during the night ended the conversation with, "Have a nice day." When I remonstrated that this wish was, to say the least, inappropriate, she actually thanked me for having called this to her attention, saying that she had never really thought about the meaning of those words and would never do that again. Certainly no Russian nurse would ever say "Have a nice day" to someone who had just lost her mother.

The smiling waiter in an American restaurant who says "Enjoy!" when setting down a dish in front of a customer is also not uttering an order or using an imperative, as some Russians think. This is an elliptical way of saying, "I hope that you will enjoy this dish." The intonation of the word "enjoy," usually uttered with a slight rise on the last syllable, makes it crystal clear that this is an expression of hope, not an order. This expression is similar to «Приятного аппетита», a contraction from «Желаю Вам приятного аппетита», the Russian version of "Bon appétit."

"Here you go!" often said by a waiter placing a dish in front of a diner is also a contraction of a longer message. Having misinterpreted this as meaning "You're leaving!", one Russian loudly declared, "No, I'm not going anywhere, I intend to eat this steak!" The phrase, however, merely means, "Now you've been served. / Your food is here. / You can now set about eating this." In other words, "Here you go now, from waiting and talking, to eating your dinner." Similarly, "Drive safely" is not an order as Russians sometimes tend to think, but the contraction of the friendly suggestion/hope, "I do hope that you will drive safely and have a good trip."

As one observer commented, «У представителей более сдержанных наций от этой беспредельной жизнерадостности довольно скоро начинает сводить скулы. Европейца она способна довести до состояния душевной неуравновешанности.»[34] While that may be the case, some may still find bright smiles and good wishes—albeit obviously superficial—preferable to the opposite extreme of blatant rudeness.

What types of people do Americans and Russians see as "positive"? The values people hold to and the words used to describe individuals differ significantly. Americans are inevitably struck by the role moral judgments, "moral passions," and "moral orientation" play in the Russian assessment of others.[35] For an American, the impression a person makes rather than personal qualities or character traits is important. Someone an American likes is "nice," a word that conveys more about how the individual relates to others than about his own qualities. Yet the American assessment, "He's a nice person," is a much stronger statement than what is implied by the literal Russian translation, «Он приятный человек.» For an American, a nice person is what a Russian means by «хороший» or «добрый». In English "He's a fine person" conveys the notion of «хороший».

«Он добрый человек» could be rendered in English as "He's a very fine person," or "a wonderful/great/extremely kind/considerate person," or "a fine and very kind person." "He's a good person" is not used all that frequently. «Он прекрасный человек» has a moral edge lacking in the English translation "She's great." But "She's a wonderful person" does have that sense.

For many Russians, the quality of being a «добрый» or «хороший человек» is far more important than many other traits such as intelligence, talent (artistic, athletic, etc.), education, common sense, or tactfulness. «Добрый» suggests kindness, good intentions, "good-hearted," "kind-hearted," "open-hearted," "well-intentioned," and has more of a philosophical tinge, while «хороший» leans more toward "morally upright," "reliable," "honest," "helpful."

«Он веселый человек» should not be translated as "He's a cheerful person" or "He's a very positive person." "He's always upbeat/in a good mood," or "He's got a great sense of humor" would be better. "Gay" should never be used to render «веселый» since in English it now has virtually only the meaning of "homosexual."

The Russian phrase «А он—ничего!» should be translated as a relatively positive assessment in English—"He's OK" or "He's all right"—but would not be positive in a literal translation. One Russian translated this in reference to an acquaintance as, "He is a nothing" (but the English meaning of that phrase in Russian would be «Он ничтожество»).

In describing an individual, the word "character" is used differently in English than in Russian. The English phrase "He's a real character" means «Он странный тип» in Russian. In English, "a person of good character" is a formal/legal description, e.g., a court witness is a "person of good character," a landlord looks for renters "of good character." An English speaker would not say of a strong or weak person, "He has a weak/gentle character," but "He's very gentle," or "He's a weak person," or "He's weak." When describing someone's character or nature, «мягкий» should not be translated as "soft." "Extremely gentle" would do it.

A common error caused by misinterpretation of American positive language is visible in the incorrect use by Russian speakers of the much abused word "OK/okay."[36] Though it does convey the sense of "fine," or "all right," as in answer to the question "How are things?"—"Everything's fine / Everything's OK"—Russians frequently assume that this common word *always* means something positive, e.g., "yes," "all right," or "I agree with you." In many cases, it does, as in answer to the question, "So we'll meet this evening at 6:00?"—"OK, see you then"; or when used in a request with the expectation of a positive answer, corresponding to the Russian «ничего, если…».

> *"Is it OK with you if Helen joins us?"*
> *"Of course that's OK. I'll be glad to see her."*
> (Конечно, буду рад с ней повидаться.)

While "OK" can mean «ничего» and «нормально», it does not always mean that something is wonderful (прекрасно):

> *"How are you today?"*
> *"Well I'm OK, but lately I've been terribly busy and I'm a bit tired."*

"How was the movie?"

*"It was OK (nothing special). / It was an OK movie
but I'm really not crazy about it."*

"OK" can also indicate conditional agreement, contingent on a factor that must be taken into account:

"I've got to go out now. I'll be back in half an hour."

*"OK, but be sure to be back by 3:30, or we'll miss the
train."*

The repetition of "OK" can sometimes convey the speaker's irritation or dissatisfaction, a negative note that Russian speakers may fail to catch:

"Will you pick up the laundry on your way home?"

"OK, OK, you've already told me twice to do that."

While Russians generally interpret "OK" as indicating agreement, it can also be used as an interrogative, meaning "Did you understand what I said?" (Понятно?). A Russian trying to obtain a tourist visa to Caracas arrived at the Venezuelan consulate in a large U.S. city to find that the building was closed. "It's open from ten to twelve, OK?" the guard informed him. "No, that's not OK," the Russian replied. "I need a visa." The guard's "OK" did not mean that he was asking for and expecting agreement from the speaker, but that he was requesting verbal verification that the message had gotten across, which in Russian would be, «Ясно? Понятно?»

Yet another linguistic reflection of the American positive attitude can cause confusion. If someone on the street slips and falls, a Russian may ask «Вам помочь?» Or, on seeing a person clutching at his chest, a Russian may ask «Вам плохо?» In a similar situation, however, an American nearly always inquires, "Are you OK?" or "Are you all right?" putting the question in a positive form to someone who is obviously not "OK" or "all right."

Along the same lines, the use of «конечно» (*of course*) also leads to misunderstanding, since the Russian word is far less forceful. In response to questions such as "Shall we meet for a drink at 5:00?" or "Will the report be ready tomorrow morning?" the literal translation of «конечно» into English, "Of course!" makes the speaker sound annoyed or indignant. A more appropriate answer would be "Yes/Sure/Absolutely, I'd love to do that" or "Sure/absolutely, it will be ready." The problem here is that while «конечно» can indicate an enthusiastic affirmative—«Конечно, я это сделаю!» (*Of course I'll do that! / I'll be glad to do that!*)—it can also imply that the speaker is asking about something obvious or self-evident. In the latter case, "of course" can sound brusque or offensive:

American:	*"Is this a good movie?"*
Russian:	*"Of course!"*
American:	*"Is it still playing in the movie theater around the corner?"*
Russian:	*"Of course!"*

In these examples the «конечно», "of course," sounds to the English speaker like "What dumb questions you're asking!" rather than like affirmative answers.[37]

The use of the positive word "friend"—and the very concept of a "friend"—differ greatly in Russian and English. In fact, as the American psycholinguist David Katan has noted, "the meaning of the word 'friend' and the expected and reciprocal rights and the duties will vary according to cultural orientation. The word itself should not be translated but mediated."[38] For a Russian, the word involves an ever-present moral obligation, while for an American, a friend can be someone with whom he went to school but hasn't seen in twenty years, someone with whom he plays golf once a month, someone he occasionally sees in church, or a really close friend. He may talk about a party where he "made five new friends." The word "friend" in English does not involve the notion of moral obligation to the other person that is inherent in Russian, to "always be there for him," even at three o'clock in the morning, someone to whom he can pour out his soul, in whom he has absolute trust. For an American, this is someone with whom one has fun, relaxes—«отдыхает» in Russian. A friend for an American is often someone with whom he engages in a specific activity rather than someone in whom he confides or with whom he shares his innermost thoughts. A «знакомый» is an "acquaintance," but there is no English equivalent for the category of friends «приятель», in between a close friend (друг) and an acquaintance (знакомый), someone with whom one is on very good and friendly terms though he is not part of your "inner circle."

Another aspect of American positive culture that is—or perhaps we will now have to say was—strongly reflected in the language is the tendency to be honest and straightforward. Unless there are solid grounds for doubt, many Americans still tend to assume that most people are speaking the truth. Hence the nationwide to-do and shock at the elaborate verbal fabrications, truth-twisting, and outright lies engaged in by people such as Bernard Madoff, former President Clinton, and a host of high-placed business executives, such as those involved in the Enron and MCI scandals. While Americans understand perfectly well that these individuals are lying—and sometimes brazenly so—no matter how many people are engaged in warping the truth, the national sentiment is that "this is not supposed to happen."[39] The rapid growth in recent years in what is known as a "cheating culture"—lying in business deals, inflating resumes, deceiving a spouse, white lies that expand into full-scale falsehoods, constant fibbing for reasons ranging from avoiding hurting people's feelings to "self-preservation"— is a relatively new development that still makes most Americans very uncomfortable.[40] After all, the most famous statement of the founding father of the United States, George Washington, known to every school child, is his "I cannot tell a lie—I did," in answer to the question of who had chopped down the cherry tree.[41]

In English it is very difficult to make the distinction between «вранье» and «ложь», a difference clear to any Russian. Perhaps closest to «вранье» are "fibbing," "a tall tale," or "a white lie."[42] For Russians, though, this word may have the implication of deliberate nonsense or twaddle, which is not the case for "fibbing." Nor does "fib" communicate the notion of exaggeration sometimes implicit in «вранье», the notion that the speaker is not telling the truth and the interlocutor is quite aware of this, and is possibly even enjoying the situation. This is totally alien to the American mentality. Great care should be taken when translating «врать» (*to lie*), as it may frequently mean merely "to be mistaken" or "to be in error."

> Где он живет? В Бостоне—вру, в Вашингтоне.
> *Where does he live? In Boston—No, … I'm mistaken /*
> *that's wrong / sorry … —I mean Washington.*

This has nothing to do with lying. An error in the translation here could prove highly offensive to a Russian speaker who meant no harm whatsoever.

If you assume that people are basically telling the truth most of the time, lies become serious business. The decades of the Soviet era produced a culture of lies, in which the leadership lied to the people and—in self-defense—people then lied to their bosses, colleagues, and associates. The culture of lying in the USSR was so pervasive that one Russian émigré critic wondered, «Может быть, мы принципиально не способны говорить правду.»[43] "Lies" and "You're lying," are very strong words and serious accusations. Though «Это неправда» or «Вы говорите неправду» theoretically can be translated as "That's a lie" (ложь), in many cases the phrase simply means "That's wrong," "That isn't so," "That's not the case," or "That's not true" (much milder then "That's a lie"). Saying, "This is not the truth" is guaranteed to annoy the English-speaking listener both grammatically and morally. The accusation "You're lying" can only mean that the interlocutor is deliberately telling an untruth, and will be taken as a strong insult. Unless the Russian speaker wishes to accuse someone of a deliberate falsehood, «Вы говорите неправду» is better translated in any of the following ways: "That's not so. / That's not the case. / That's not true. / I think you're wrong. / I think you're in error. / I think you're mistaken." The polite American expression low-level bureaucrats often use when questioning the truth of a client's assertion—"I don't doubt your word but"—e.g., that you made a reservation in this hotel or ordered a ticket on this flight—often actually means, "That's all very nice and you may well be telling the truth, but since the computer has no record of your order, you're not going to get that reservation/flight. Sorry about that!"

Americans generally aren't willing to lie for their friends, even when asked for help. Most Americans are extremely unwilling to tell an untruth regarding a friend's professional experience to help him get a job, or to write a recommendation containing false information. They will hesitate to fill out an application for a bank loan or a college application containing false information since they are quite aware of the extremely serious consequences that threaten if these untruths are discovered.

In the last decade there has been a flood of cheating in business resulting from sheer unadulterated greed, and the intense pressure to get the high grades needed for admission to a good college or graduate school has led to a tidal wave of copying exams and papers in American high schools and universities. There has been widespread coverage of this cheating epidemic in newspapers, magazines, and online. Yet the verb «списать с» (to copy from/off someone else's exam paper—or nowadays from one's smartphone) has no idiomatic equivalent in English, and cheating on exams and copying off someone else's paper is still considered anathema by the majority of Americans. That ingrained distaste for cheating is the product not of a self-righteous sense of morality, but of the notion inculcated from earliest childhood that you must "do your own work" and "think for yourself." American individualist society is devoid of the deeprooted culture of the collective still present in Russia, the imperative need to help out a friend by letting him copy from you. For a Russian to refuse someone permission to copy a test would be considered uncomradely, unfriendly, and just plain selfish. In the U.S. in the 1950s and 1960s not only was cheating in high schools or colleges punishable by expulsion, but in many educational institutions "honor codes" stipulated that failure to report an observed incident of cheating was a punishable offense. When I taught Russian literature to a class of Russian émigrés at a New York college they were dumbfounded by my refusal to let them sit next to each other to easily copy off their neighbor's papers. "But, Elena Vladimirovna," one student wailed, "You're one of us! How can you do that? We're all friends! That's not fair!" It was difficult to explain that my American upbringing and values won hands down over my Russian background and Russian concepts of the collective, friendship, and comradeship. They reacted with amazement to the information that in an American high school or college both parties involved—the one doing the copying and the one allowing his friend to copy—risked severe penalties and even expulsion from school.

Though nowadays American positive thinking regarding doing your own work and the sacrosanct principle of telling nothing but the truth often fall victim to the pressures of a highly competitive society, the classic belief in positive thinking is still very much part and parcel of American ideology and daily life.

3.

Think Negative
~

If Russians are shocked by unflagging American smiles, Americans are often put off by what they perceive as persistent Russian pessimism, negativism, and a fatalistic attitude to life. As one Russian writer put it:

> Средний русский—это меланхолик, который надеется на лучшее, одновременно тщательно готовясь к худшему. Часто для такой стратегии есть достаточно оснований. «Вот так со мной всегда!»—печально восклицает русский, когда его постигает очередная неудача ... Такой здоровый пессимизм нередко помогает русским избежать катастрофы.[44]

The reasons for such pessimism go well beyond the scope of this book. While for years Americans were influenced by the tradition of positive thinking, hard work, and rewards for that work—as defined by the Protestant ethic—and by life in a country free from foreign invasions and totalitarianism, Russians were subjected to decades of revolution, civil war, famine, the Stalin purges, totalitarian dictatorship, and the horrors of World War II. In an atmosphere where the individual's interests were constantly subordinated to those of the state, with "fate" (or «судьба», as the Russians like to call it) dealing out one blow after another, it was unthinkable for all but the most naïve citizens to remain blindly optimistic. That pessimism became ingrained as a trait of the national character, justified by decades—indeed centuries—of tribulations that optimistic, positive-thinking Americans have never experienced. What is of interest here is how that pessimism has been reflected in the language.

Several recent studies have shown that the positive thinking dominating the American mentality may not necessarily be an unmitigated boon. Visualizing a positive outcome and the inevitable achievement of goals in any and all situations may in fact blunt the ambition of many individuals to reach those objectives; reiterating positive feelings about the self—"I am lovable" and "My life is joyful"—may in fact impact negatively on those suffering from low self-esteem.[45]

Russians, however, tend to see the future as a series of negative scenarios, a world-view determined by their country's history. In Soviet times a repressive and authoritarian system, inflexible bureaucracy, and constant shortages meant that individuals were blocked from achieving their goals or from hoping for a positive outcome. It was far less disappointing to assume that a project was destined to fail and then to be pleasantly surprised if things did in fact "work out." The superstitions deeply ingrained in Russian culture posit that it is better to think negatively to ward off "the evil eye" and not to jinx an outcome by being too positive, e.g. "This trip will probably be awful," rather than "I'm sure we'll have a wonderful time."

The American mentality, which has little sympathy for dwelling on failures, setbacks or «неудачи», is directly opposed to the Russian world-view. This issue is central to the Western Judeo-Christian tradition of sympathy and compassion for those who are in need or suffering. In America bad news must be gotten over quickly in order to find a solution to problems, to move forward and get back to positive thinking. Do you have to fire a subordinate? Get it over with as quickly as possible. You'll get back to work, and he'll go about finding a job. Did the doctor just say you have an incurable disease? Get out of his office as quickly as possible. He has to see his next patient, and you need to decide on a course of treatment and get your affairs in order. Time is money.

No «неудача» is seen as lasting. The American attitude is "better luck next time" (не повезло сегодня, повезет завтра). That holds true for both professional and private life. So what if you got fired from your job? The next one will probably be more interesting and pay better. And if you're divorced following a bad marriage? "It's always better the second time around."

The Russian attitude to bad news and misfortune is the exact opposite. No matter what, a Russian doctor will avoid telling a patient that he is doomed, and will communicate the bad news to one of the sick person's relatives. In a country beset for centuries by misfortunes and disaster, however, sympathy and empathy for the sufferer are universally accepted, and the American attitude seems cold or unfeeling.

In Russia a «неудачник» or "loser" does not get the kind of sympathy bestowed on him in the U.S. Well-meaning Russians who try to console a downcast American with an English version of «Ах ты бедненький» or «бедный мой!» are likely to be sharply rebuffed. These expressions are linguistic clichés in Russia, but since no American wants to be an object of pity, a proper translation of this sentiment is extremely difficult. A common Russian expression of sympathy and understanding, «бедненький» (literally, "*you poor one*") makes no grammatical or emotional sense in English, and usually evokes a highly negative reaction. A better expression of sympathy in English is, "You poor thing," immediately followed by an expression of optimism such as "I'm sure you'll manage/come through this all right/be fine" (similar to Russian expressions such as «Ах ты, бедняжка, но ничего, ничего, все пройдет ...»). The American response to the poor soul who makes the rounds of his friends seeking a shoulder to cry on is, "He's got to get his act together." "Success breeds success,"—and whining does not. A setback is overcome by taking action, not by passive acceptance.

The language used to describe "negative" or "bad" people differs in English and Russian. «Он плохой человек» can be rendered as "He's no good," rather than as "He's a bad person." «Злой человек» combines a series of possible meanings including "nasty," "evil," "bad," "malicious," "unpleasant," and "unkind." Care should be taken to avoid automatically using dictionary definitions of these words. «Он злой»—the opposite of «он добрый»—has no single, clear translation in English. If you say, "He's a bad person," "He's evil," or "He's a nasty person," you will only be reinforcing the stereotypes most Americans have of Russians after reading a

Dostoyevsky novel (in translation) in college. For the first sentence of Dostoevsky's *Notes from the Underground*, in which the narrator describes himself as a «злой человек», translators have come up with ten different ways of saying that someone is "bad news"—evil, nasty, mean, spiteful, nasty, malicious, malevolent, angry, to name only a few.[46]

English has a much milder view of the concept of «злой». A simple solution would be "He's awful," or, more commonly, "He's mean." "He's not a (very) nice person," "He's no good," or, colloquially, "He's a nasty piece of business" or "He's bad news," are also possibilities. In such constructions the word "person" is usually dropped. «Он тяжелый человек» means that the individual is "a difficult case," "hard/tough/rough to deal with." In English, and more generally, in American society, the moral passion which infuses «Он злой» or «Он добрый» is totally lacking. Americans simply do not get as excited as Russians over these particular character traits.

The grammatical structure of the Russian language, which makes much greater use of negative constructions than does English, helps to create this impression of a negative mindset. Another major factor is the linguistic legacy of the Soviet era, which created an elaborate bureaucratic jargon, a "culture of bans" covering a range of ideas, actions, and types of behavior that were discouraged, proscribed, or punished. These collective fears wove into the fabric of the language a whole tier of everyday negative expressions, idioms, and clichés. Though with the advent of perestroika these phrases gradually lost their force and sense of intimidation, this combination of grammatical structure and the negative culture of bans and prohibitions created an impression of the Russian language as one based on the word «нет», and of Russia as an authoritarian dictatorship.

In the 1960s and 1970s the American image of a Russian was close to a negative caricature, the picture of a Soviet who responded to any question with either «нет» or "Is not possible" (нельзя). U.S. diplomats and journalists often referred to the former Soviet minister of foreign affairs, Andrei Gromyko, as "Mr. Nyet." American visitors to Russia found that almost everything they wanted to do evoked a response of one of two negative words: either «нельзя» or «некультурно». The latter word had very different meanings for the two cultures, and (in literal translation) was an endless source of humor for Americans. «Вести себя некультурно» was perfectly clear in a Russian context, but in American English one does not talk about behaving in an "uncultured" manner. In the U.S. it was not considered "uncultured" to wear coats inside public buildings or theaters, to put one's feet up on a chair, call people immediately by their first names, eat during class, or wear tattered jeans. Moreover, the «некультурные дети Дяди Сэма» wondered how they could be accused of a lack of culture by denizens of a country in which people mercilessly pummeled each other in overcrowded subway stations, salesgirls barked at customers, and eating a piece of potato off the end of a knife was common behavior at table. But certain aspects of common American body language, such as putting one's feet up on an office desk, going shoeless (without putting on slippers—«тапочки») or even barefoot at home, can seem highly «некультурно» to many Russians. Though the Soviet period is behind us, both Russians and Americans are still occasionally surprised at what each side considers as acceptable or unacceptable behavior.

Far more confusing to Americans than issues of what is «некультурно» are the endless number of other Russian "don'ts"—«нельзя», or other words and phrases beginning with the particle «не». Interpreters and translators frequently attempt to avoid excessively literal translation of «нет», «нельзя», and «невозможно», for these and a plethora of other Russian negative expressions helped create in the West an image of Russians as stubborn, aggressive, gloomy, and pessimistic—all qualities intrinsically opposed to those valued in the American national character. In regard to this question of negation and a negative attitude, the issue of social norms must be distinguished from the question of the structure and grammar of the Russian language, a tongue extremely rich in negative words and expressions.

Prohibitions, warnings, and expressions indicating what one cannot/should not/must not do are voiced quite differently in Russian and English. Many negative constructions need reworking in English if an English-speaking Russian is to avoid sounding like "Mr. Nyet." Correctly rendered, these "don'ts" should sound less categorical in English than in Russian.

The word «нельзя» has several shades of meaning. It can mean that something is impossible and cannot be done: «*Нельзя лететь без пересадки из Мадрида в Москву*» can be rendered as "There's no direct flight between Madrid and Moscow," or "You can't fly direct between Madrid and Moscow." (In rendering such impersonal constructions English prefers to make "you" rather than "one" the subject, another common Russian error.)

«*Нельзя* здесь переходить улицу—вот подземный переход» is not "It is not possible to cross the street here," since physically it is indeed possible to do that. Such a sentence should not be translated as "It is not permitted," "It is not allowed," or "It is forbidden," all grammatically and stylistically unfortunate choices which reinforce the negative "iiz not pawsseeble" stereotype of Russians. Options include "You can't cross the street here" or "There's no pedestrian crossing here" or "You can't get across here." Saying, "Don't cross the street here," while a warning—there may well be bad consequences if you do—can sound like an order rather than well-meaning advice. «*Нельзя*» can also indicate that something is impossible for legal reasons: «*Нельзя* в Россию без визы.» Or that the prohibition is for moral reasons: «*Нельзя* выходить на улицу в этом пдатье—это просто неприлично.» It can also be a translation of "don't—no way!" Someone attempting to stop a child from swallowing a pencil eraser might well yell «Ваня, *нельзя*!».

Depending on context, the word «невозможно» requires different translations. In the following examples there is no indication of a prohibition; rather, the sentences point to impossibilities.

> Здесь *невозожно* говорить из-за шума.
> *You can't talk / It's impossible to talk / It's impossible to make yourself heard … here because of the noise.*

> Я бы очень хотела в Вам присоединиться, но у меня столько работы, что это *невозможно*.
> *I'd really like/love to join you, but I've got so much work that … there's no way I can make it / I really can't make it / I just can't make it / it's just not possible.*

Other negative expressions which require reworking in translation include «не следует», «не рекомендуется», «не положено», «не надо», and не нужно». Under the Soviet regime, hortative expressions such as «не следует, не рекомендуется, не надо» often had a distinctly "political" or slightly menacing undertone, implying that doing whatever might entail some very unpleasant consequences. Though today the political implication is usually lacking, there is still an implicit warning of undesirable consequences of the subject's actions: yes, you physically can do this, but you are taking your chances. For example: «*Не следует* Вам писать диссертацию на эту тему, по ней уже столько написано.*» "It is not recommended" is not an advisable rendering. Better translations would be: *I would (really) not advise you to / I would not suggest that you / It wouldn't be a good idea for you to … write on this topic.*

In English the Russian impersonal construction is replaced by a pronominal subject. Additional examples include:

> *Не следует* пить холодный сок после горячего чая—заболит горло.
> *Don't have / Don't drink / It's not a good idea to drink / You're taking a chance if you drink … cold juice after hot tea—you can/could get a sore throat.*

> *Не рекомендуется* много есть на голодный желудок.
> *Eating on an empty stomach is not a good idea. / It's not a good idea to eat a lot on an empty stomach.*

«Не надо» and «не нужно» are warnings or admonishments suggesting that an action should be avoided. «Не надо» has a stronger, more imperative tone. The meaning is often best rendered as "Don't do it!" rather than by a literal translation such as "It is not necessary" or "It is not needed." The phrase clearly implies that there may be negative consequences to doing something.[47] Or take the following examples:

Не надо давать шоколад ребенку—он его плохо
переносит.
*Don't give the child any chocolate—he has trouble
digesting it properly. / That child shouldn't eat
chocolate—he doesn't digest it properly.*

Не надо здесь бегать!
No running allowed here! / Don't run here!

Не надо ему говорить, что он плохо говорит
по-русски—у него нет способностей к
иностранным языкам. Он только обидится.
*There's no need to tell him / There's no point in telling
him / Don't tell him … that he speaks Russian badly.*

«*Не надо* мне никакой помощи! Сам справлюсь с
этим заданием!»
*I don't need/want any help! I'll … deal/cope with this
problem on my own / take care of this problem by
myself!*

Не надо каждый день говорить мне, что тебе
нужны деньги! Я прекрасно это помню.
*Stop / Quit / There's no point in / You don't have to
keep … telling me every day that you need money!*

Не надо сейчас звонить Маше! Мы опаздываем
в театр! Don't even think about calling Masha! We're
already late to the theater!*

Не надо волноваться—все наладится.
*Don't worry …—it will be all right / —everything will
work out.*

«Не надо» can also serve to indicate "No, thank you," a rejection or
refusal of something:

«Вам помочь?»—«Спасибо, (ничего) *не надо*. Все
в порядке».
*"Do you need help?" "No, thank you. ... I'm OK. / I'm
all right."*

*"Do you need a hand?" "No, thank you. ...
Everything's under control. / Everything's fine."*

«Показать Вам где этот магазин? »
«Нет, *не надо*, сам найду.»
"Want me to show you where this store is?"
"No, thanks, I'll find it myself."

The expression «не нужно», though very close in meaning to «не
надо», does not have the imperative sense of the latter. It is slightly
less categorical. The basic English meaning is "there is no need to,"
rather than "it is not necessary."

Мне больше *не нужно* ходить в библиотеку.
У меня дома уже есть все материалы для
диссертации.
*I don't need / There's no need for me ... to go to the
library any more.*

Мне *не нужно* сейчас печь пироги. У нас
остались пироги со вчерашнего приема гостей.
*There's no need to bake / There's no point in baking / I
don't need to bake ... any more cakes right now. We've
got one left over from last night's party/reception.*

The expression «не положено» conveys the sense that something
"contravenes rules/regulations / is not accepted / is not done."

Почему я не могу войти к директору без доклада?
Не положено.
*Why can't I come to see the director without an
appointment?*
*Those are the rules. / I'm afraid that you can't do that.
/ Unfortunately, you can't do that. / That's the way
things are done here.*

Эта премия Вам *не положена*—она
предназначается только двум категориям
служащих.
*You're not eligible for that bonus—it's only
given/awarded to two categories of staff/workers.*

Sometimes the meaning of «не положено» is close to that of «не
принято», meaning that certain accepted norms of behavior or
etiquette will be violated by the proposed behavior:

Не положено выпить, пока король не сделает
первого глотка.
*The guests are not supposed to / You are not supposed
to / One doesn't … drink until the king makes the first
toast.*

Не положено так громко говорить в метро.
*You're not supposed to / People don't/shouldn't … talk
so loudly in the subway.*

If an action is related to a more informal custom or to generally
accepted patterns of behavior, «не принято» will be translated
slightly differently from «не положено» (but not as "it is not
accepted"):

В Америке *не принято* есть торт ложкой—всегда
пользуются вилкой.
*In America … cake is not eaten with a spoon; it is
eaten with a fork. / we don't eat cake with a spoon; we
use a fork.*

Не принято сразу обращаться к человеку по имени.
*Don't call people by their first name right away. /
We don't use first names right away.*

For both Russians and Americans, the word «неудобный» is
a frequent cause of linguistic and cultural confusion. In its literal
sense the word is easy to translate. A «*неудобный* поезд» that

leaves at 6 o'clock in the morning is an "inconvenient train," a «*неудобное* кресло» with a hard seat and back is an "uncomfortable chair," and «*неудобная* одежда» means "uncomfortable clothes." When «неудобно» means "awkward," however, the translations "uncomfortable" or "inconvenient" do not always work. These are very common errors of Russian speakers. «Мне *неудобно* звонить твоему приятелю—профессору кафедры математики» is not, "It is … inconvenient / not convenient … for me to call your friend the math professor," but rather:

> *I feel awkward / I don't feel comfortable / I don't feel quite right … about calling your friend.*
>
> *I'm not sure it's right for me to call your friend.*

Colloquially, one can say, "I feel funny about calling him."

In a sentence such as «*Неудобно* звонить Смирновым после десяти вечера—они очень рано ложатся спать», «неудобно» is not "inconvenient." The sentence can be rendered as "Please don't / I wouldn't … call the Smirnovs after ten since they usually go to bed early."

The answer «Ну, это *неудобно*» to the question «Можно ли зайти к господину Смирнову завтра в десять часов?» can be rendered as "That's not a very good time," or "That's a bad time for him," meaning that the caller should make an appointment at some other time.

«Он живет в доме, расположенном далеко от метро. Это так *неудобно*» can be translated as "His house is far from the subway. That's really … very inconvenient / a nuisance / a problem." In English "inconvenient" takes a modifier such as "really/very/quite" much more often than «неудобно» does in Russian. In the British film *The Russia House*, based on Le Carré's novel, one character asks his interpreter why Russian acquaintances are constantly saying "This is not convenient," and learns that in fact they are trying to say "this is not proper."[48]

This word «неудобный» has caused countless misunderstandings. If an American gives a Russian the phone number of a friend or colleague who may be able to assist him in some way, and tells him to call, it is up to the Russian to do so—and to do so soon.

If the Russian does not, then both the American and his friend will feel that they have been put upon for no good reason. Saying to the American «Мне *неудобно* ему звонить» will annoy him and make him feel his time has been wasted. If you're not going to call, why did I bother my friend? It is expected that someone interested in a job or a favor will do the phoning himself, and that it is not up to the American to call on the Russian's behalf. Nor is it «неудобно» or «нескромно» to stress your qualifications on the phone. That, after all, is why you are calling.

The common words «неприятность» and «неприятный» should not automatically be translated as "unpleasant," since that is often not what the Russian speaker is trying to say. Someone's «неприятности» may be his "problems" or "troubles." «У него на работе сейчас большие неприятности» should be rendered as "He's got a lot of problems." or "He's in real trouble right now at work." A few other examples:[49]

> Конечно, это *неприятный* момент, его придется учесть.
> *This is a difficulty/problem/annoyance/irritant … we will have to take into account / with which we will have to cope/contend / that we will have to face.*
>
> Спад цен на эти акции—*неприятный* момент для нашей фирмы.
> *The decline/drop in the prices of these stocks is … causing problems/difficulties for our firm / a negative factor for our firm.*
>
> Для него эти факты оказались весьма неприятными.
> *These facts/events/things … were highly embarrassing for him / put him in a very uncomfortable/awkward position.*

In a reversal of Russian linguistic negativism, the word «проблема» (*problem*) always implies something negative in English, though this is not necessarily the case in Russian. In both languages, the word indicates a situation or dilemma requiring a solution. In certain contexts, however, the Russian word means an "issue" or a "question" rather than a "problem." At multi-national conferences Americans are frequently surprised to hear from Russian colleagues that there is a need to «решить целый ряд *проблем*», when the Western participants were quite unaware of the existence of any "problems." The Russian suggestion in fact indicates a wish to discuss what in English would be a number of "issues," "questions," "subjects," "topics," "agenda items," or "elements for discussion." For English speakers "problems" unequivocally points to issues on which there are major differences of opinion.

The adjective «неудачный» and the verb form «не удалось» have also been frequent sources of misunderstanding for many of the Russian-American couples I interviewed for my book on Russian-American marriages.[50] Statements by a Russian spouse about a movie or a play that the couple had seen, such as «Этот фильм *неудачный*» or «режиссеру явно *не удался*» when rendered in English as "This film was not successful" or "The director did not succeed," were highly annoying to the American spouse. For a speaker of American English, this implied a sweeping value judgment based on "inside knowledge"—by whose standards did the film "not succeed"? Succeed in doing what? An idiomatic translation of the word does not require the use of "successful" or the idea of "success": "This wasn't a good film." / "This film didn't work." / "The director didn't pull this one off." / "The director didn't do a good job on this one."[51]

In many cases, where American English tends to think positively, Russian prefers a negative construction. Rendering these in English as negatives will sound both awkward and pessimistic.

Не исчезай! / Не пропадай!
Stay in touch!

Не кладите трубку!
Hold on!

Больше не болейте.
Stay well.

По газонам не ходить.
Keep off the grass.

Мы Вас ждем с нетерпением.
Wrong: *We're waiting to see you impatiently.*
Suggestions: *We're looking forward to seeing you. /*
                      We're eager to see you.

Sometimes the negative form is tantamount to an under-statement that must be made explicit. «Это *небесполезно*» can be "This is useful" or "This is quite useful." «Он *невысокий*» is far stronger than "he's not tall"; it means "he's short." «Он *небедный*» is a sarcastic way of saying "he's extremely well off."[52] Or take «Он *неглупый*», which means "he's quite intelligent" (literally, he's not stupid). It can be a bit hard, though, as one British observer of the Russian scene has pointed out, to translate a negation of a negative as a positive: «Он очень *неглупый* человек», literally "He's a very not stupid person," in fact means "He's extremely bright."[53]
Several common Russian negative idioms may be expressed by either positive or neutral phrases in English:

Наши деловые партнеры *не случайно* включили этот момент в контракт.
There are good reasons why / It is with good reason that / It stands to reason that / It is no surprise that / It is understandable why / We can understand why / It is not fortuitous that … our business partners included this point/element in the contract.

Ни для кого не секрет, что она его любовница.
Everyone knows / It's perfectly clear to everyone / It's an open secret … that she's his mistress.

Посторонним вход *запрещен*
Private property (sometimes: "*No trespassing.*")

The phrase «не один» leads to a *contresens* when mistranslated as a negative:

Не одному поколению эмигрантов пришлось приспосабливаться к американскому образу жизни.

This does *not* mean:
> "*Not one / Not a single ... generation has had to adapt to American life.*"

But rather:
> "*Many generations / More than one generation ... has had to adapt to life in America.*"

But:
> *Ни одному человеку не* пришлось ждать в очереди.
> *No one / Not a single person ... had to wait in line.*

The same kinds of errors often occur when translating «не раз»:

Я *не раз* говорил Вам, что мы этого не сделаем.

Wrong: *I told you not one time, that we will not do this.*

Right: *I've told you ... over and over / many times / time and time again ... that we will not do this.*

Double negatives in Russian are often best translated as positives:

Нельзя не видеть сложности этой проблемы.

Very awkward:
> *It is not possible not to see the complexity of the problem.*

Possible translations:
> *The complexity of the problem should not be overlooked/ignored.*

> *We cannot fail to see / We cannot ignore ... the complexity of the problem.*

Better (positive) translations:
The complexity of this problem must be taken into account.

We must deal with / We must face / We must come to grips with / We must tackle … the complexity/ difficulties of this problem.

Мы **не** можем **не** обращать внимания на этот вопрос.
We must / We should / We are called on to / It is our duty to … pay attention to this issue/question.

Another difficulty is posed by the huge number of questions that are asked in the negative in Russian, but that are couched in positive terms in English:

Не скажете ли мне, как пройти до станции метро?

Wrong: *Could you not tell me how to get to the subway?*

Right: *Could you please tell me how to get to the subway.*

Excuse me, could you tell me how to get to the subway.

Could you (kindly) tell me where the subway is?

"Please" or "excuse me" are necessary when asking this kind of question. In Russian, the interrogative form «не скажете ли» softens the question and automatically makes it polite, but in English the interrogative construction does not do that, and using a literal translation from Russian, "Won't you tell me?" can sound odd. Americans are often amused by the Russian question «Вы не скажите, сколько времени» and by the answer, «Не скажу». To the English speaker this sounds as though the speaker were saying, "Yes, I do know what time it is, but I won't tell you" (because I don't like the way you look / because I'm in a hurry / because I feel like being nasty). «У Вас случайно *не будет* ручки?» can be turned into a polite English request by adding the modal "would" or "might." Rather than "do you have," a better form would be "Excuse me, would you have a pen?" or "Would you (happen to) have a pen? "

Such "negative" questions, which are in fact requests rather than questions, require reworking in English if they are to be comprehensible and polite. Take «*Не могли бы* Вы налить мне кофе?» or «*Не передашь* мне молоко?». In English the negative particle must be dropped, and a "word of politeness" included:

> *Could you <u>please</u> give me / Could I <u>please</u> have …*
> *some coffee?*
> *Could you <u>please</u> pass (me) the milk?*

The failure to include the word "please" in such requests is a major reason why Russians frequently sound rude to Americans. In Russian, however, the negative form of the request accompanied by the conditional particle «бы» eliminates the need for «пожалуйста». In fact, the excessive use of «пожалуйста» instead of "negative construction + бы" when asking a question is one of the characteristic errors made by Americans speaking Russian, just as the failure to use "please" marks "Russian English."

The requests «*не можете ли* Вы?», «*не могли бы* Вы?», «Вам *не трудно*?», «Вас *не затруднит*?», «*Не трудно ли* Вам?», and «*нельзя ли*?» can all be rendered by "could you please/kindly …," or "could/may I bother/trouble you to …"

Advice that is phrased in the negative in Russian is often positive in English:

> *Не сделать ли* Вам …
> *What if you were to … / What about your doing … /*
> *Perhaps you might do … / Perhaps you might think of*
> *doing …*

One of the most common "negative" Russian words, «ничего», is frequently mistranslated in English:

Как сегодня погода?
Погода сегодня *ничего*.
The weather today is … OK / quite all right.

Or:

Погода *не ахти* какая (но вполне приличная для прогулки).
The weather is … not so great / not so wonderful / so-so … but fine for a walk / but it's OK for a walk / but it'll do for a walk.

Как она тебе?
Ничего, приятная женщина
How did you like her?
She's OK / nice / a pleasant lady/woman.

Многие рассказы этого автора, по-моему, очень даже *ничего*.
I rather like some of that author's stories. / I think some of that author's stories are OK/interesting/quite good.

Ничего подобного.
No, nothing of the sort. / No, I meant something quite different.

Извините, я опоздал.
Ничего, не страшно.
Never mind. / It doesn't matter. / Don't worry. / Don't give it another thought. / Forget about it.

На столе было много превосходных вин, а мне *ничего* нельзя!
There were many excellent/good wines, but I can't … have any / try any / drink / have a drop.

The words «нечего», «никто/некто», «никуда», «некуда/негде», «никогда», and «некогда» do not always come across correctly in translation, as the expressions "*nothing,*" "*nowhere to* go," and "*nothing to do*" do not always fit the same way into Russian and English sentences.

Делать *нечего*, придется ехать сейчас, а то опаздаем.
Nothing doing, we've got to go (right now), or we'll be late.

От *нечего* делать он стал читать детективный роман.
Out of boredom / Since he had nothing else to do ... he started reading the detective novel.

(Не)*чего* греха таить. Это я виноват—часы остановились.
To tell the truth / To be frank / I must admit that ... my watch stopped.

Возразить *нечего*, я согласен. Работа отличная.
I'm in full agreement. / I agree completely. / I have no objections. / I have nothing to add. ... It's an excellent ... piece of work / job.

Никто здесь про него *ничего не* знает.
No one here knows anything about him.

Я заблудилась в лесу. *Не у кого* было спросить, где дорога/тропинка!
I got lost in the woods, and there was no one to ask how to get back to the road/path!

Мой старый велосипед *никуда* не годится—у него сломано колесо.
My old bicycle is ... no good / good for nothing / damaged ...—it has a broken wheel.

В зале было столько народу—сесть *негде*.
There were so many people in the room that ... there weren't enough seats / some people had to stand / you couldn't sit down.

Я *никогда не* знаю, куда ему звонить.
I never know where to call/reach him.

Я так занята, вздохнуть *некогда*.
I'm so busy. / I'm so swamped. / I don't have a free
minute. / I don't know if I'm coming or going.

It takes time to get used to the idiomatic equivalents in English for these Russian expressions. Of course, English has negative expressions, but they are generally expressed in a less categorical and more polite form than in Russian. And remember—while expressions of negation are sometimes necessary, in America, think positive!

4.

Think Active or Passive?
~

Differences in the way languages and cultures use the active and passive mood are reflected in vocabulary, idioms, and grammatical constructions. The psycholinguist David Katan has noted that, "Cultures ... vary in their perception of the environment: some may feel that they can control the environment ... and feel in charge of their own destiny."[54] In the world-view of some cultures, the environment and human life are subject to forces over which man has no control. Commonly recurring key words and phrases related to these forces—fate, destiny, luck, chance, providence, acts of God, or *force majeure*—tell us a great deal about a culture. America is a prime example of a culture that feels it controls its own destiny. In a society based on individualism, each person bears ultimate responsibility for his life and actions. The phrase "the buck stops here"[55] emphasizes that an individual must take personal responsibility for his actions, and cannot assign responsibility to someone else or to external forces. An American psychiatrist once recounted how a man who had lost his job came to see her because he was convinced that he alone, not the economy or other forces beyond his control, was responsible for this situation. According to the psychiatrist:

> The assumption of personal responsibility for ill
> fortune is endemic in our culture ... These people
> ... seem to have a hard time with the idea of fate or,
> to put it less grandly, with acknowledging that many

> life events are beyond our control ... Bad outcomes,
> in such a system, bespeak personal inadequacy.
> Often, at this juncture, people turn to psychiatrists
> in the hope that 'self-knowledge' will remedy
> things. The virtues associated with accepting fate—
> endurance, dignity, discipline, perseverance—are
> barely in our cultural lexicon.[56]

As the American saying goes, no matter what happens, no matter how disastrous the situation, "Don't just stand there, *do* something!"

In a country of climatic extremes, the efforts of Americans to control even the weather are striking examples of such attempts to master their environment. An American journalist wrote:

> To city dwellers even rain can be perceived as an
> affront, both personal and civic ... What good
> is technology, we seem to believe, if we cannot
> prevent natural forces from interfering with human
> purposes and disrupting the social order? The idea
> of acquiescing to, or even enjoying, blizzards, heat
> waves and all of our climate's other insults is at
> the very least un-American. So we overheat and
> overcool ...[57]

"If I want to fly from New York to Atlanta, why should a snowstorm that morning prevent me from doing that! What do you mean, my flight's been cancelled? Put me on another plane!" That is a typical American reaction. Trying to exert maximum control over one's life and "our romance with our own invincibility and our sense of the crucial importance of our every moment and desire"[58] (perhaps slightly tempered by the vulnerability felt in the wake of the terrorist attacks of September 11, 2001) are quintessentially American.

The languages of cultures in which people do not believe they have extensive control over their environment contain a range of key words and phrases expressing a sense of fatalism, such as the Arabic "In sha Allah" (*God willing*). Russian abounds in popular sayings such as «Бабушка надвое сказала», «Человек предполагает, Бог располагает», «Это вилами на воде писано». In America quite different expressions on this subject are popular: "The Lord helps those who help themselves," or "Where there's a will there's a way." As a Russian observer commented:

> Большинство американцев не верят в силу
> судьбы, а слово «фаталист» в американском
> варианте имеет негативную коннотацию. В
> американской культуре естественным считается
> контроль над ситуацией, и если человек
> полагается на судьбу, то его будут рассматривать
> как ленивого и безынициативного.[59]

In America a "fatalist" is considered to be a passive, lazy individual, and the adjectives "fatal" and "fateful" foretell bad things to come. «Смертельная болезнь» is a "fatal" illness, "fateful" is rendered by the gloomy Russian epithets «роковой» and «судьбоносный», as in "September 11 was a fateful day for Americans." A Russian student, commenting on the American rejection of fatalism and the attitude of "think positive" said that:

> Americans don't believe in the power of fate and
> being called fatalistic is one of the worst criticisms
> one can receive. What does that mean? In my
> opinion they simply try to be optimistic, and don't
> fall under the influence of misfortunes. They tend to
> avoid misfortunes by keeping control over whatever
> might potentially affect them. They evaluate positive
> changes and have a future orientation also because
> they don't like fixing their minds on bad news.[60]

The word «судьба», together with such words as «душа» and «тоска», has been described as one of the Russian concepts shaping the language's semantic universe. «Судьба» stresses a passive, negative dimension of human activity and life, the irrational and unpredictable nature of human existence, the irreversibility of what is already predestined.[61] In America, however, the linguistic-cultural universe stresses the active, positive, rational, and predictable nature of an individual's life. While "fate" is applied to individual episodes—"I guess he was fated not to get that job" or "She was not fated to marry him"—in Russian the concept frequently refers to a person's entire life and implies a strong degree of predetermination.[62] It is certainly true, as the psycholinguist Anna Wierzbicka has pointed out, that:

> the idea of Fate with a capital F is inimical to the spirit of capitalism. Drive towards action, free enterprise, initiative, striving for individual success in life, competition—all these things are hard to reconcile with the idea that one's life does not depend on one's own efforts.[63]

To indicate a positive fate English uses the word "destiny," e.g., "It was his destiny (he was destined) to be elected President," "From childhood on all her friends knew that it was her destiny (she was destined) to have a great career on the stage." The expression "Manifest Destiny" is used to describe the early American push from the east to the west coast, the belief that Americans were "destined" to control the entire continent.

In Russian, however, there is no such word for a "fate with a positive outcome." (The rather dated word «рок» is even bleaker in meaning.) Fate is seen as irreversible and inexorable: «судьба» is «неминуемая», «неотвратимая», «неумолимая», «неизбежная» and cannot be changed.

Man has no choice. «От судьбы не уйдешь», «Двум судьбам не бывать, а одной не миновать» state the Russian proverbs. Any native Russian speaker can easily produce dozens of expressions with «судьба»: «зависеть от судьбы», «какими судьбами», «жаловаться на судьбу», «быть обиженным судьбой», and many others.[64] Life is «в руках судьбы», events occur «волею судьбы». Though these pose no particular difficulties for translation—e.g., «неумолимая судьба» is "inexorable/relentless fate"—Americans basically do not think in such terms, diametrically opposed to their conviction that the individual, and not some kind of «слепая судьба», is rationally responsible for his actions and, above all, for their consequences. As a result, English is filled with active constructions and active verbs embodying the philosophy of positive thinking. For a Russian, «судьба» is a fate very often associated with negative events, as illustrated by the following joke which, though it can be translated word for word into English, will not be understood by an American, for whom this concept of "negative fate" is alien:

Разговаривают два мужика:
Ты знаешь, что такое судьба?
Знаю. Это когда идешь по улице, а тебе прямо на голову падает кирпич.
А если он упадет рядом?
Значит, не судьба![65]

The differences in attitude, shouldering personal responsibility vs. giving in to fate—active vs. passive—are clearly reflected in the use of language. Russian has far more constructions than English indicating states or actions in which something is done to the subject rather than conditions in which he himself does something. Numerous Russian phrases with the dative case, modal words such as «можно», «нельзя», negative infinitive constructions without modals (не бывать, не видать), reflexive verbs (не спится, не работается), and impersonal expressions emphasize the subject's passivity and inability to control his environment. Though today's younger generation of Russians is starting to move away from this kind of pessimistic determinism, negation still remains deeply ingrained in Russian linguistic structure and idioms.

Russian folklore is rich in examples of negation + infinitive + dative which indicate that the individual is powerless to counteract fate: «Не видать тебе этих подарков …» and «Не видать Егорю отца-матери …».[66]

In English translation, a whole range of common Russian expressions using the dative case and/or a reflexive verb and/or infinitive + бы and/or impersonal expressions require an active subject:

Мне холодно. *I'm cold. / I'm feeling cold.*
Ей хорошо. *She's fine / OK / doing well / all right.*
Мне скучно. *I'm bored.*

Ему спать хочется. *He's sleepy.*

Отдохнуть бы.   *I'd like to … relax / get some rest / take some time off.*

Failure to restructure these Russian idioms in English leads to some very common errors:

1. «Мне скучно» is "I'm bored," not "I'm boring"—which means «Я скучный человек». An individual who is boring is a "bore," e.g. "That professor is a real bore—you can fall asleep during his lectures." A sentence such as «Не ходи на этот фильм! Скука смертная!» can be rendered as "Don't go to see that film! / Forget about that film! … It's a real bore. / You'll die of boredom. / It's so boring."

2. «Мне интересно» means "I'm interested," not "I'm interesting" which translates as «Я интересный».

3. Russian speakers often confuse "tired" and "tiring." For the expression «ему спать хочется» or «он устал» be sure to say, "He is tired," not "He is tiring." There is a major difference in meaning here:

Let's put off the next round of golf—the players are clearly tiring.
Давайте отложим следующий раунд гольфа— игроки явно устают.

I think he's tiring the audience with that lengthy speech.
Боюсь, что он утомляет публику своим долгим выступлением.

He's an extremely tiring and boring speaker.
Он страшно занудный и скучный докладчик.

Russian impersonal constructions may be translated with an active subject: «Вдруг послышался шум» (*Suddenly I/we heard a noise.*) If the identity of the subject is unclear, however, a passive construction can be used: "Suddenly a noise was heard." One of the first rules in any English writing class is, however, to avoid the passive whenever possible, and in general English prefers active to passive mood.

> Хочется с кем-то поговорить
> *I'd like to talk / I am in the mood to talk / I feel like talking … to someone.*

> Пить хочется.
> *I want a drink. / I'd like to drink something. /*
> *I'm thirsty.*

> Ей не спится.
> *She's not sleepy. / She doesn't feel sleepy. / She doesn't feel like sleeping.*

This passive construction can also indicate an inability to do what one would like to do or must do:

> Мне завтра рано вставать, легла в десять часов, а никак не спится.
> *I've got to get up early tomorrow, I went to bed at 10:00, and just can't … get to sleep / fall asleep.*

> Мне завтра надо сдать отчет, уже поздно, а никак не получается.
> *My report is due / I've got to hand in the report / The deadline for my report is … tomorrow, and it's late, but I'm having real trouble writing.*

> Нам здесь живется очень плохо, квартира крохотная, но мы не можем оставить больную мать.
> *Things are very difficult for us / Life is really tough/ rough for us / We're having a really hard time … here and the apartment is tiny, but we've got to stay with (we can't leave) our sick mother.*

Where Russian uses impersonal constructions, English requires a subject for the verb:

> Светает.
> *Dawn is breaking. / It's daybreak.*

> В марте в парке уже зеленеет.
> *By March the leaves are … coming out on the trees / already green.*
> *The trees in the park are already green and it's only March.*

Context often determines the choice of words and of an active or passive construction:

> Мне совестно.
> *I'm feeling guilty that … / I feel bad about … / I feel awful that … / I'm embarrassed/upset that …*

> Вам весело, а ему так плохо! Он же потерял работу, а Вам все равно—думаете только о себе!
> *You couldn't care less / You're just fine / You're enjoying yourself / You're in a great mood / You're in great shape / You're having a great/good/fine old time / You're doing great … but he's lost his job and is … really miserable / in really bad/ terrible shape / in real trouble / having a terrible time of it.*

> Ему было трудно понять чего, собственно, она от него хотела.
> *He was having a hard time understanding / It was difficult/hard for him to understand / He was having difficulty understanding/grasping … what exactly she wanted from him.*

> Его было трудно понять.
> *He was hard/difficult to understand.* (i.e. because he had a strong accent in English)

Тебе обидно?
Are you hurt/offended/upset?

Мне в конце концов удалось убедить его в том,
что нужно доучиться и только после этого
поступать на работу.
*I finally … was able to convince him that / managed
to persuade/convince him that / succeeded in
persuading/convincing him that / got him to see that /
made him see/realize that*

Кошелек потерялся—ну, так случилось.
I lost my wallet (literally, *the wallet got lost*) —*well,
things just happen that way.*

Я вчера собрался на вечер, но не получилось,
как-то не сложилось.
*I was planning to come to the party, but things just
didn't work out.*

Почему они разошлись?
Как-то не сложилось.
Why did they divorce?
Things somehow didn't work out.[67]

Such impersonal constructions with the dative case and/or reflexive
verbs have been interpreted as reflecting a Russian tendency to
respond passively due to the conviction that many phenomena are
subject to «судьба» rather than to human control.

The common Russian expression «Ну что (же) мне делать?»,
often uttered with hands spread apart in the air, expressing
helplessness and the inability to take action to counteract судьбу
(*fate*), is not popular with Americans. It can convey several shades
of meaning:

What can I do about this?
What am I to do about this?

> *So what should I do?*
> *(So) what on earth should/can I do (about this?)*
> *(So) what am I supposed to do about this?*

The implicit answer is often "There is nothing I can possibly do about this, so why are you asking me?" This kind of rhetorical despair does not evoke sympathy from action-oriented Americans. If, however, the speaker is really asking the interlocutor what he should do, and not merely looking for sympathy, the question should be phrased as:

> *What would you like me to do about this?*
> *What would you suggest I do?*
> *What do you want me to do?*

An American inquiring as to what he should do about a problem expects a concrete answer. He will not ask this question rhetorically (А что же мне делать?!), implying that "(You and) I know that there is nothing I can or will do." Since the American is trying to determine what he *can* do in this situation, he will quickly lose respect for anyone with an attitude of «ну, что же мне делать!»

The whole series of Russian proverbs and sayings asserting that one must try to «обмануть судьбу» "to be quiet, patient, passive, and stay in the background and refrain from action or work" is alien to the American way of thinking and to the Protestant work ethic. For example:

> Тише едешь—дальше будешь.
> Поспешишь—людей насмешишь.
> Моя хата с краю.
> Работа не волк/Работа не медведь—в лес не убежит.

Concepts such as «авось проскочу» or «вера в удачу» are also foreign to the American "go get it"/"do-it-yourself" attitude.

The idea behind «авось», "*Well, perhaps we can count on luck since things are so unpredictable*," sounds very odd to Americans. This notion of «повезло / везет / не повезло /не везет» is used far more often in Russian than in English. English refers to "a stroke of luck" or "a streak of bad luck," but the outcome in a given situation primarily depends on the speaker's actions, and not on luck or fate. «Вдруг повезет» (*Maybe you'll be lucky*) is usually used only in situations such as:

a. Your friend is buying a lottery ticket. "Well, maybe you'll be lucky!"

b. It's snowing and most flights out of New York are being cancelled. Your friend has a ticket that evening to Moscow. "Well, maybe you'll be lucky!"

c. Your friend has gone out with several girls but each one has left him for another man. Tonight he's going on a blind date with his friend and her girlfriend, whom he hasn't yet met. "Well, maybe tonight you'll be lucky!"

"He never has any luck" is a reasonable translation of «Ему постоянно не везет», but this "loser" is not someone with whom Americans will want to spend much time. Saying «Мне не везет» is generally not going to gain much sympathy or respect from Americans.

These differences in languages and culture are particularly important for questions of linguistic-cultural behavior and etiquette.

5.

Etiquette and Behavior
∽

Nothing is harder for a foreigner to grasp than the unspoken and unwritten rules of etiquette and behavior in a foreign culture, and then to comply with them, day in and day out. The best-intentioned foreigner who ignores this framework of rules for behavior risks misunderstanding and hurt feelings. Customs, habit, politeness and decorum, norms and standards are all part and parcel of behavior and etiquette.[68] American behavior is predicated on unstated norms of privacy, personal space, and the presentation of a positive image of the self to the outside world.[69] Of course, a huge tome could be written on the difficulties Americans have in grasping what constitutes acceptable behavior in Russia, but that is a different subject.

The most elementary behavioral speech acts include salutations, introductions, inquiries as to how the other party is feeling, compliments, invitations, congratulations, expressions of gratitude, excuses, apologies, and leave-taking. The well-known American sociologist and analyst of human interaction Erving Goffman summed this up neatly: "Through all of these, the recipient is told that he is not an island unto himself and that others are, or seek to be, involved with him and his personal private concerns … The individual must phrase his own concerns and feelings and interests in such a way as to make these maximally useable by the others as a source of appropriate involvement."[70]

The informality commonly associated with America sometimes leads people to believe the dangerous misconception that in the U.S.

"anything goes" in terms of behavior. Most of the time Americans don't have to give conscious thought to "what goes," but foreigners are faced with daily choices. The most serious mistakes—and yet the ones hardest for both foreigners and Americans to grasp— are those that result from a literal translation or transfer of what would be acceptable behavior in the foreign culture onto American soil. While the intentions are the best, the reactions evoked by such behavior can be incomprehensible to both Russians and Americans.

Yet failure to observe the unwritten and subtle rules of accepted behavior in the U.S. can seriously impact business and personal relations. Theoretically, in a democratic society a cleaning woman should be treated with the same respect as the boss. While this is clearly not always the case, the average American still expects that in daily life situations he will be treated politely and as an equal.

Addressing Someone

The first step in social interaction comes with addressing someone— i.e., what you call him or her. It is a truism that Americans tend to go on first-name terms much faster than Russians, that here "the democratic idea" makes itself felt. Bosses and subordinates often address each other by first name; so do people you have never met who are trying to sell you something on the phone. At a first meeting, however, if an American addresses a Russian as "Mr. Ivanov," the response should be, "Mr. Smith," until Mr. Smith either says, "Call me Jim" or calls his interlocutor "Igor." When writing, the abbreviation "Mr." is *always* used.

Russians sometimes err in addressing people as "Mr." or "Miss" + the first name, e.g., "Mr. Jim" or "Miss Ellen" or "Mrs. Jane." Often these forms are used because Russians have seen them in British or American literature. But such forms of address, used by nineteenth-century slaves and servants when speaking to their masters, are now a thing of the past. In a modern novel about an American in love with a Russian girl, the hero, laughing at the memory, recounts to his American friends that when he was in Moscow, "I was respected. Russians often called me 'Mr. Daniel'"—his first name.[71] In talking to a stranger, a man can always be addressed as "Sir." But if "Mr." is the chosen form of address, then the last name *must* be used: "Mr. Johnson, I'd like to talk to you for a moment."

Addressing an unknown woman as "Miss" is always acceptable. For example, this form of address is commonly used with service personnel such as a waitress—"Miss, I'd like a small orange juice, please, and whole wheat toast," or with a secretary, "Miss, I'd like to leave a message for Mr. Johnson." When speaking to an older woman, "Madam" (with stress on the first syllable) or "Ma'am" is acceptable. "Mrs."—the form of address for a married woman, as opposed to "Miss" for an unmarried woman or a female stranger—should only be used with the last name: "Mrs. Johnson, please see the manager." (This question of how to address a woman presents problems in Russian, too, for the long-used «девушка» (literally "*girl*") sounds rather odd when the lady in question could be a grandmother, and modern Russian is still struggling to come up with an appropriate substitute.)

The word "guys" (and also "girls" and "kids") is frequently overused by Russians trying to show off their knowledge of colloquial English. The word "guys" has become increasingly popular—particularly among young people—when addressing a group of both men and women, since English does not have an accepted informal way of addressing a mixed group. The word is so informal, however, that it can be insulting to older, educated people. "You guys want to go for a beer?" is no way to address a group of professional colleagues. Neither is "You folks," another colloquial word used to refer to both men and women, and one that has gained in popularity through use by politicians talking to "all you folks out there." Coming from a foreigner, both words will sound rather strange. A more neutral form of address to a mixed group, "Would (all of) you like to go (out) for a beer?" is preferable. Here today's Russians and Americans are encountering similar problems, as «ребята» (*kids*) would be inappropriate for a group of older people, and the demise of «товарищ» (*comrade*) and «гражданин» (*citizen*) have left big gaps in forms of address. The formal form of address to a group of men and women is "Ladies and Gentlemen" but that is usually reserved for speeches or formal announcements.

As opposed to Russian, in which they are quite common, words such as "boy," "girl," or "woman," are never used as forms of address in the U.S. A very small child can be informally addressed as "dear," "honey," or "sweetie," but these words should never be used in talking to a woman—regardless of her age—unless she is a very close friend. Otherwise this may sound like a form of sexual harassment. Russians often try to use such endearments to compensate for the lack of diminutives and of the familiar form for "*you*" (ты) in English, but this is not a good idea.

Asking how someone is feeling

In most cases, the American who asks "how are you?" is barely listening to the answer. The phrase functions more as a greeting than as a genuine question, and the response, as noted by a Russian observer, is very different from what a Russian would say in answering a similar query:

> Если вы встретите на улице знакомого русского и неосмотрительно спросите, как он поживает, он остановится, наберет в грудь воздуха и примется самым детальным образом просвещать вас.
>
> Он перечислит все свои недуги и недуги своей жены; расскажет, что случилось после того, как он последовал совету врача; вы узнаете, как он чувствует себя в данный момент; он сообщит вам, каковы школьные успехи его сына и что сказала учительница на последнем родительском собрании.
>
> Никогда, никогда не спрашивайте русского, как он поживает, если вы на самом деле не хотите знать, выспался ли он и что он съел сегодня на завтрак.[72]

For Americans, there is only one standard response to "Hello/Hi, how are you?" and that is "Fine, and you?" Variants of "fine" include "OK," "Pretty well," and "Great." "I'm good," an expression which has become very common, should be avoided. Despite its popularity, this expression is grammatically wrong, and can also sound perilously close to «я хороший человек». Another common meaning of "I'm good" is "I'm OK, don't need help," as in, "Are you all right with that heavy suitcase?" "Thanks, I'm good."[73]

Another frequent Russian response to the question of how one is doing is «Нормально» (*normal*). The Russian word, however, does not convey the idea inherent in "normal." The closest rendering of «нормально» would be "OK, I guess," or "Not bad." The following are some examples of dialogues translating «нормально»:

«Как твоя спина? Не лучше?»
«Нормально.»
"How's your back doing?"
"OK/Fine."

«Хорошо съездил к родственникам?»
«Нормально».
"Did you have a good time with your relatives?"
"Sure, everything was fine."

Он вел себя нормально
He behaved very well.

Это вполне нормально
This is perfectly natural (not normal).

«Как провели вечер»?
«Нормально».
"How was the evening?"
"Fine/OK."

Americans enjoy promoting both their own positive images and those of their friends. If someone has been given a promotion at work, won the lottery, or published a book, his friends will be genuinely happy for him and sincerely share in his joy at this success. Jealousy of someone else's good fortune is not a characteristically American trait. "I'm really glad for you" or "How nice for you" are the commonly accepted and appropriate reaction to someone's good news.

All these questions and answers are usually very time-limited in English. Brevity and a short duration of communication characterize what Edward Hall calls "low-context" cultures such as the U.S., vs. "high-context" cultures such as Russia.[74] In the latter cultures, communication is more time-consuming and more indirect, and a speaker may not immediately get to the point the way he does in English.

Other versions of "How are you?" include "How are things? / What's up? / How's life (treating you?) / How are you doing? / What's new?" These purely informal questions do not require any kind of detailed answer.

The answer "fine" is often used even by people who are not at all "fine"—someone who has lost his job, whose child is ill, or whose house has just been damaged by fire. An American will generally only share with a close friend that, "Well, I've been having some problems lately," or colloquially, that things are "not so great/ hot." If the situation is really awful, he may say "Pretty bad/lousy." Otherwise, the answer is "fine," followed by a short explanation. For example, if his mother has been rather ill: "Well, we've been having a few problems lately. My mother hasn't been feeling so well." Or "Well, actually/in fact, I've been a bit under the weather with the flu, but I'm feeling better."

"I've got a bad cold" or at worst "I've been having some health problems recently" is about as much information as most Americans will care to communicate. The kind of detailed medical bulletin many Russians provide in response to such questions will not be received with great enthusiasm. A Russian, however, finds it absolutely normal to go into detail on health problems, will expect sympathy from a listener, and will be extremely sympathetic to his interlocutor's health and illness issues.

«Я плохо себя чувствую» can be rendered by "I'm not feeling well" (never "I'm feeling badly"), or "I'm feeling a bit low." If things are really very bad, «Чувствую себя скверно», the answer to "How are you?" could be "I'm feeling rotten." If the problem is more emotional/psychological than physical, such as «Я не в духе», then "I'm in the dumps" or "I'm feeling a bit out of sorts" will do.

For positive-thinking Americans, people with whom one wants to associate are by definition individuals who are doing "fine." The Russian verb «я болею», with the possibly lengthy period of poor health which it implies—as opposed to «я болен»—does not have a clear equivalent in English. Americans do not go around saying, "I am sick." «… В Америке принято во всех случаях жизни казаться бодрым, здоровым, благополучным», noted one

Russian commentator.[75] As one doctor remarked, "Whether you're a celebrity or an ordinary person, it's obligatory, no matter how badly you're feeling, to display optimism publicly."[76] Casual and business acquaintances do not spend much time on those who are sick. In many workplaces there is strong internal psychological and external pressure from bosses and colleagues not to call in sick, and an employee is unlikely to regale all his colleagues with stories of his illness.

Short answers are customary in reply to specific questions regarding an illness: "I've got a bad cold" or "I've sprained an ankle." Too many such inquiries may be seen as an annoying invasion of privacy. In cases of serious illness, unless the interlocutor is a close friend or someone the person knows well, "I've been having some medical problems" is an acceptable answer. There is no need whatsoever to inform him, as one might in Russia, about all the home remedies that your grandmother always recommended for this ailment. Seeking sympathy and advice, a sick Russian will often talk nonstop about symptoms and treatment, not so in the U.S.[77]

Cultural differences also exist regarding specific health problems. Americans do not generally discuss their blood pressure «давление», a common topic of conversation for most Russians.

And very many Russians are convinced that the barometric pressure has a strong impact on blood pressure, leading to considerable confusion in conversations with Americans, for whom these two kinds of pressure are totally separate issues. Statements by Russians to Americans such as "It's going to rain, I feel my pressure changing" will be greeted by an uncomprehending stare. Unless he is a meteorologist, the American will have no idea of what the Russian means to say.

Nor is discussion of one's personal «давление» common. «У меня подскочило давление» will not encounter much understanding or sympathy. If an American has high or low blood pressure he goes to the doctor, gets a prescription for an appropriate medication, and does not trumpet this news to all and sundry.

While the statement «У меня плохо с сердцем» is clear to any Russian, Americans do not usually say, "I'm having heart/cardiac problems." An American will interpret a Russian saying this as meaning that such a problem is a very serious one, as anything involving cardiac issues usually points to a serious illness, not to feeling under the weather. Nor will «печенка побаливает» be understood. Americans do not go around complaining of "liver pain." Rather, they complain about their sinuses, colds, and arthritis. While they may have no idea of their blood pressure figures, Americans can recite their cholesterol levels in their sleep. To the shock of many Russians, American women are quite frank about «месячные дела»—"I'm having my period," "It's that time of month," or "I'm having bad cramps today"—all subjects off limits for most Russians.

In talking to someone who has recovered from an illness and is looking well, an appropriate comment is "You're looking great/wonderful." But great care should be used in attempting to render «Вы поправились» in English. Yes, the expression means "you're looking better," but it also means that the person has put on weight, perhaps a leftover from the Russian decades of famine and starvation resulting from wars, bad harvests, and decimated populations. For an American, however, any indication that a few extra pounds are now hanging around will not be taken well; it is a compliment, though, to say to someone, "Tom, you're really looking good, you've lost weight." In general, as one anthropologist noted, "Looking thin is a sign of great acceptability in the culture."[78] In the U.S., as the saying goes, "You can't be too thin or too rich."

On meeting strangers at a cocktail party or a reception, the question Americans often ask is, "What do you do?" This is a completely acceptable way of starting a conversation, a quick way of ferreting out an individual's profession, and may indirectly provide information regarding the person's income level. A Russian, however, might begin the conversation with "Where are you working?" In the U.S., however, salaries and income are not proper subjects for conversation. Many Americans would be more frank in responding to a question about their sex lives than about their finances.

Encountering an acquaintance

«Тысячу лет не виделись/сколько лет, сколько зим» can be rendered in English as "I haven't seen you in/for ages!" or, very colloquially, "Long time no see." The standard phrase of greeting,

"I'm so glad to see you!" usually has no more emotional force than "How are you?"

While you are talking to your American acquaintance, John Smith, along comes your friend, Harold Jones, who greets you with a friendly "Hello." Answering him with "Hello, how are you," you *immediately* introduce him to John Smith—"John, this is my friend/colleague Harold Jones." While in Russia it is not obligatory to introduce a third party who has happened to join a brief conversation, in America it is considered rude not to introduce the person, even if it is perfectly clear that he will not be staying on to continue the conversation.

«Очень приятно», the Russian expression used when being introduced to someone is rendered in English as, "Nice/Pleased to meet you." If it turns out that «мы уже знакомы», the answer is "We've met." And when taking leave, the phrase "Pleased to meet/ have met you" should be said to the new acquaintance—even though neither party may be at all pleased and it is highly unlikely that they will ever meet again.

If Americans bump into each other at the office many times during the day they will at least say hello and smile on each occasion. Russians, however, feel that they have earned the right to ignore someone's presence if they have greeted him earlier in the day, and no one would find such silence rude.

Phone and meeting etiquette

The expected niceties in phone conversations differ radically in Russia and America. In the U.S., if someone other than the person you wish to speak to answers the phone, the correct response is, "May I speak to Mr. X?" or "Could I please speak to Mr. X?" In Russia, the request might be "Ivanov, please," or simply "Give me Ivanov."

In America, the answer, either on the phone or if waiting in someone's office, is often, "He'll be with you right away." That means precisely that: in a few minutes, not in half an hour. But in Moscow, a response may be «сейчас», which, though it translates literally as "right away," may mean an undefined amount of time. If Mr. Ivanov is going to see you «сейчас», the wait may range up to fifteen or twenty minutes. The Russian concept of time is much more elastic and fluid than in the U.S. «Сейчас» repeated twice is always encouraging, usually indicating what an American would mean by "right away."

There can also be confusion with the English and Russian versions of the expressions "He's away from his desk" or "He's stepped out." These correspond to the Russian «Он вышел», meaning "He's not here now, but he'll be back." «Его сегодня нет и не будет» means "He's not in today and won't be coming in," while «Он ушел» means either "He's not in the office right now because he's gone off somewhere for quite some time," or "He's left for the day." American secretaries often may give more specific explanations than do Russians as to why someone is unavailable: "He's in a meeting/conference. / He's with a client now. / He's not available now. / He's tied up now. / He's out of the office for half an hour. / He's out to lunch."

In a situation when it is not clear what someone has said it is perfectly acceptable to ask: "Could you please repeat the question? / I'm afraid I didn't get that, could I bother you to repeat it? / Would you mind repeating that?" Russian speakers, however, frequently just say "Repeat" or "Repeat, please," which would be quite acceptable in Russian, but can sound a bit abrasive in English.

When calling with an important request or a matter of substance an American often asks, "Is this a good time for you?" (Вам сейчас удобно говорить?). If it's not a good time, the answer may be, "Well, I've got someone in my office. / I'm leaving in ten minutes for the airport. / We actually just sat down to dinner." A correct reply is "When would be a good time to talk?" In Russian, however, the caller would suggest that he and the party he is calling should «созвониться», a verb for which there is no direct translation in English. The meaning is "We will call each other, " but since this does not specify who will call whom it can be extremely confusing and often irritating for time-conscious Americans, and there can be considerable delays when the Russian caller and the person called each wait for the other to call back. In the U.S. it is always made *very* clear who is to call whom. Will I call you tomorrow morning, or will you call me? And at what time?

On the other hand, there is no direct Russian equivalent for the American phrase "I'll get back to you," which does not imply that the person will do so that same day, since then he would have specified the time of the call. This sentence can also be used as a brush-off, to indicate that the individual is not particularly interested in calling you back.

At the end of a conversation an American often says, "We should get together." That "should," however, contains no indication of obligation, of «должно» or «нужно». This is a purely empty phrase, with a meaning that runs the gamut from "I'd love to see you soon," to "I hope I never see you again." Such a use of "should" is similar to the use of "must," as in "You *must* come visit us soon," "You *must* meet my friend Mr. Jones," or "You really *must* try this piece of chocolate cake," all non-binding expressions of a suggestion or intention, not an order.

Another commonly accepted phrase that does not have a Russian equivalent with the same implications is "Let's have lunch." In Russia, this would mean a serious intention of getting together soon over a midday meal. In the U.S., if there is a suggestion of a specific time—"Next week / My secretary will call you / What day would be good for you for lunch?" —the speaker is indicating a serious intention of meeting with the other person. Otherwise, as one commentator notes, the phrase is:

> not a serious invitation to have lunch but simply a casual way of saying "good-bye." The invitation is no more than to say something like, "I've enjoyed the conversation and wouldn't mind getting together sometime." The person who expects this utterance to be followed by another communication setting up the actual luncheon will be frustrated by this apparently broken dialogicality.[79]

The fact that the U.S. is a low-context culture, in which brevity is valued, results in certain differences in phone etiquette, in particular for business calls. Once the person needed is finally on the phone, an American does not like to waste time. A lengthy digression on the weather or family matters prior to stating the reason for the call, behavior that would be acceptable and even polite in Russia as a good introduction to the matter at hand, may irritate an American, and too many such "niceties" may be followed by a curt "What can I do for you?"

Parting dialogue

Though as a rule American phone communications are char-
acterized by brevity, people in the U.S. generally spend more
time than Russians in saying good-bye at the end of a phone
conversation. As the anthropologist Margaret Visser has noted:

> Telephone conversations—where words are
> everything because there are no external signs to
> help in making judgments, and facial expressions
> cannot be seen—have evolved elaborate rituals
> for verbally ending an exchange without offense.
> Cutting off the other person without warning is very
> rude, and especially to be guarded against because
> hanging up is so easy to do. Thanking-as-an-ending
> is brought into play as a preparation for hanging up,
> and often offered twice or three times during the
> ending ritual.[80]

In Russia, however, even after extremely long conversations, the
actual end to the talk may be fairly abrupt by American standards.
It is not customary in Russian to use the equivalents of phrases
such as "It was nice talking to you. I really should be going/running
along." "I won't keep you" would be rendered in Russian as «Не
буду Вас задерживать». In the U.S. it is usually not appropriate
to sign off with "Bye now, ciao," (Ну все, я пошел/пока) without a
few prior words indicating that a farewell is coming. "Hope to see
you soon. / Thanks for your time/trouble. / I'll be seeing you. / We'll
be in touch. / Stay well. / Good-bye (sometimes shortened to "Bye"
or "Bye now")" are more common wind-ups to a conversation.

"See you later," which has no real meaning, can be confusing to
Russians. This casual way of saying "good-bye" may make a Russian
think that he and the American will actually be meeting later again
that day or in the very near future. The same holds true for another
casual form of taking leave with no Russian equivalent, "Take care"
(a version of «всего хорошего»).

A Russian saying, "I wish you success," (Желаю удачи), which
does not sound idiomatic, is simply expressing his good wishes to

his interlocutor for everything he may be doing. English tends to prefer either "good luck," or "all the best," or to voice a more specific wish: "I wish you every success in your work."

Sending regards to someone can be done in several ways. In Russian, this would be «Сердечный»/«привет» (от меня) Ивану/ Кляняйтесь Ивану …» While in Russian these «приветы» are taken seriously and are usually in fact conveyed to the addressee, in American culture the attitude to sending "regards" is by far more casual. Few people would be offended or even notice if X did not send regards, or if Y forgot to give someone those regards.

Requests and questions

The key words in English for any kind of request—be it of a close relative, a friend, a boss, a colleague, a subordinate, or a waiter— are "please" and "thank you." Failure to use these words—especially "please"—is one of the major reasons why so many Americans consider Russians to be rude. A Russian émigré psychiatrist noted the failure of Russians to use these two words as frequently as required in English:

> Русские…,которые давно здесь живут, замечают, что вновь прибывающие как-то не очень любезны, потому что они почему-то не так часто говорят «спасибо» и «пожалуйста» … Английские "please" и "thank you" для вас пустые слова, потому что вы не говорите и не думаете на английском языке и, естественно, на нем не ощущаете.[81]

In Russian there are many ways of expressing the notion of "please" aside from «пожалуйста», which in many contexts would be inappropriate. Americans who speak (or try to speak) Russian often sound strange or even sarcastic to Russians because they keep muttering «паажаалааста» when a Russian would say «будьте добры», «будьте любезны», use a negative interrogative (не сможете ли Вы?) or a rising intonation. In English, the word "please" is virtually required when you are making a request: "*Please* give me that pen" / "Could you pass the salt, *please*?" /

"Could you *please* answer this letter?" / "May I *please* speak to Mrs. Goodman?" / "*Please* take off your coat" / "I'd like the check, *please*." Even signs prohibiting various kinds of actions are frequently phrased as requests containing "please"—"*Please* keep off the grass," or "*Please* don't feed the animals." As one linguist wrote, "In English ... 'Please' with an imperative is almost indispensable."[82] That includes conversations between bosses and subordinates, colleagues, friends, close relatives, and husbands and wives: "Miss Jones, *please* mail this letter" or "Professor Havemeyer, *please* come in and sit down." And when writing in English, do not put a comma after please in such requests: "Please come to see me at 3:00," *not* "Please, come to see me at 3:00."

In translation, some requests need a syntactic change. «Скажите мне, пожалуйста» is a common request when asking directions or in many other situations. In English, however, the literal and all-too-common translation from Russian, "Tell me, please," sounds rude or sarcastic. In Russian the use of a simple imperative is quite acceptable, without "please," and a Russian therefore feels comfortable asking "Tell me how to get to Fifth Avenue" with no additional "lubricant" words. As one Russian linguist commented, an attempt "to use a more elaborate strategy, such as 'Excuse me please, could you tell me ...' is completely counterproductive, as it often means your interlocutor is way down the street before you finish speaking. Transferred into English, such direct imperatives seem brusque and discourteous."[83] Correct English would be, "Could you please tell me (how to get to 34th Street)?" or "Excuse me, could you tell me (how to get to the zoo from here / how much these flowers cost / where Mr. Jones's office is / how to say «расписание» in English)?"

The same change from the Russian word order is needed for:

Садитесь, пожалуйста.
Please have a seat. / Please sit down.

Дайте мне, пожалуйста ...
Could you please give me ...

Принесите мне, пожалуйста ...
Please bring me ... / Could you please bring me ...

Modal verbs (could/would) in English are strong indicators of the degree of politeness inherent in a request, and since such modal verbs do not exist in Russian, a Russian risks being perceived as rude if he has not mastered these American forms. "Could" is much milder than "will." Attempts at direct translation from Russian such as, "Will you please bring me some coffee?" or "Will you please get the bread from the kitchen and put it on the table?" sound rather like an order. More polite wording would be, "I'd like," or "Could I," for example, "I'd like to have the vegetable soup," or "Could I have the vegetable soup, please?" In English, an offer of another cup of coffee—"Would you like some more coffee?" usually produces the answer "Yes, please" (and "*please*" is not optional) or "Thanks, I'd love some," or "No, thank you."

A wish or request that in Russian can be expressed through either a positive or a negative construction: «Хорошо/неплохо было бы (сделать то или другое)» in English is almost always rendered by a positive phrase: "It would be good/nice if you could please do such and such." While the Russian answer may take a negative form: «Я не против/ничего не имею против/не возражаю», in English it will once again be rendered as a positive: "That's fine with/by me."

The answer to a question may involve two or more people, e.g. "Who could help me with this problem?", in which case in English the speaker *always* puts the other person first: "Fred, John, and I will be glad to help you," *not* "I, Fred, and John." Putting yourself first is considered discourteous. And a very common mistake of Russian speakers in English is the translation of «Мы» as "we" in phrases such as «Мы с Фредом Вам поможем». This does not mean, "*We and Fred* will help you," but "*Fred and I* will help you."

In English, inquiries as to whether an interlocutor would like to do something are often phrased using modal verbs, as in "Would you like to do / Could you please do / Would you be interested in doing / How would you feel about doing ... something." Asking "Would you like a cookie?" is preferable to "Do you want a cookie?" (i.e., "If I offer you one, will you take it," rather than "Do you want one, yes or no?").[84] Other polite forms of a request are: "There's something I'd like to ask you to do / I was wondering if you might ... / It had occurred to me that you might (like to do

X / be interested in doing X) / It occurred to me that you'd be the perfect person to do X." Since such constructions are not used in Russian, Russians frequently fail to understand that such polite ways of making requests using modals, i.e. "could you/would you," ("whimperatives," as they are known to linguists) are sometimes in fact orders or demands. One Russian employee got into trouble with his American boss because he failed to realize that the man was giving orders, and not merely making suggestions when he first came out with what sounded like a very mild request, "I'd like to ask you to do this," and then, "I was wondering if you might/could/would take a look at (this report)." A professor saying "You might want to check the spelling and grammar in your essay," or "There may be some issues with the language of your essay—you might want to take a look," more often than not is saying that the writing is stuffed with both kinds of errors, a statement which in Russian would be made in so many words.[85] In America this is a way of acknowledging the addressee's independence and autonomy, of softening the imposition of one's own will on someone else.

There have been numerous such misunderstandings. For instance, Russian students responding to the request of their English teacher "Would you like to read this paragraph?" with "No, I wouldn't." During training in Houston a Russian astronaut had a conflict with his teacher and was trying to rectify the problem. "She's a bit strange," he said to his interpreter. "Yesterday, for example, she asked me whether I would like to write the exercise. I just said, 'No, let's do it orally,' but she got offended." The use of such modals as "would" or "could" mislead a Russian speaker into thinking that something is a suggestion rather than an order.

In the same vein, a guard asking "Do you want to move your car?" or "Would you mind moving your car?" is in fact giving an order, «Переставьте Вашу машину!»

The answer to a question/invitation such as "Would you come to our place for dinner next Friday?" (с большим удовольствием) is "I'd be delighted/glad to do that." or "I'd love to." The equivalents of «безусловно» or «разумеется» are "Yes, of course," or "Naturally." Invitations in English are more indirect than in Russian: "I'm having a birthday party next week. It would be lovely if you could come!" For occasions celebrating birthdays, to which Russians attach so much importance, the invitation often sounds like a demand:

«Ты обязательно должен придти!» A pressing invitation is understood as a truly sincere one and also reflects the importance of friends and hospitality in Russian culture.

If a request is refused because the individual is not able to carry it out, «Я не в силах», the English equivalent is "I'm afraid I'm not up to it/that." «Ни в коем случае!» in English is "No way!" or "Out of the question!," not "In no case."

Refusals to carry out a request, or warnings not to do something, need recasting in English:

> Этого лучше не делать.
> *Perhaps you'd better not do that. / It might be better*
> *for you not to do that.*

> Ни при каких обстоятельствах! / Об этом не
> может быть и речи!
> *(That's) out of the question!*

Since Americans try to avoid categorical or dogmatic statements or responses, even general expressions of disagreement are couched more gently in English than in Russian:

> Не могу с Вами согласиться. / С Вами не
> согласен.
> *I don't think I can / I'm afraid I can't / I don't really …*
> *agree with you.*

> Это не то, что я имел в виду.
> *That's not quite/really what I … intended / had in*
> *mind / meant.*

When answering questions on how to get to a particular place, Americans go into far more detail than do Russians. In answer to the question «Как пройти к Большому театру?» a Russian might merely say «Вон туда, прямо», while an American explaining how to get to the Metropolitan Museum will answer, "Go to the corner, turn left, walk two blocks to Fifth Avenue, turn right, cross the Avenue and you'll see it right in front of you."

Russian speakers may be confused when responding to utterances that may be perceived as questions, but are in fact declarative statements or commands. Such misunderstanding frequently occurs because of the increasing tendency in the U.S. to use a rising intonation towards the end of the sentence, an intonation that closely resembles an interrogative. "We're moving the office to the fourth <u>floor</u>?" may sound like a question, when in fact it is a statement. So too, "He got the job of <u>vice-president</u>" with a rising intonation can be mistaken for a question instead of a declaration of fact.

Asking for, giving, and receiving advice

There is a fundamental difference between asking for advice in Russia and asking for advice in the U.S. In Russian, the statement, «Я хочу с Вами посоветоваться» (*I'd like to ask for your advice*) is taken very seriously both by the person asking for advice and the person asked. There is a tacit assumption on both sides that the response will be considered carefully, since the very act of requesting advice implies respect for the person asked. Asking someone for advice can also be a way of placing ultimate responsibility for the decision on that individual, making him a party to the decision—"Well, he advised me to do that."

An American, however, may ask six people for advice and then blithely go and do whatever he pleases, completely ignoring any and all suggestions. (Americans are, after all, individualists.) No American would be offended or «обижен» because a friend or colleague had not taken his advice, and certainly would not hold him responsible for not having followed it. He might, however, be tempted to say, "I told you so," if the person failed to take his advice and subsequently things did not work out.

A Russian, on the other hand, may be quite resentful: "If you didn't take my advice, why did you bother me to ask for it?" If something did not work out, it is obviously because the friend failed to heed that advice.

In the U.S., the individual must "decide for himself," and he may therefore have a much more casual attitude about listening to the views of others. As the Russian linguist Tatyana Larina has pointed out, in Russian culture advice (asked for or unrequested) is considered not as interference in one's private life, but as help and assistance.[86] Russians on the receiving end of advice feel that this is a demonstration of goodwill and friendliness rather than an imposition or a violation of their privacy (a word which does not even exist in Russian).[87] In the U.S. advice is given using tentative and conditional phrases (put positively) such as: "If I were you ... / Perhaps you might consider ... / Why don't you try to ... / It might be a good idea to ... / What if you were to ..." The person giving advice might finish by saying one of the following phrases: "But, after all, it's up to you. / It's your decision. / That's just what I would do. / In the last analysis, it's your problem. / You've got to decide this for yourself. / You've got to live with this decision." In English the verb "to consult" is often used with the meaning of asking for advice: "I'd like to consult my thesis advisor before submitting this article to a journal" or "If she's still in pain next week she'll need to consult a neurologist."

Because Americans are so highly individualistic and independent, they usually respond badly to unsolicited advice, often viewed as a violation of their independence and privacy. You would be well advised not to tell an American friend, "If I were you ... " («Я бы на Вашем месте ...»). This has led to unfortunate situations where an American takes offense at the unsolicited advice proffered by a Russian who is only trying to be helpful and is speaking with the best of intentions, as is customary and absolutely accepted behavior in Russia.

Another common Russian habit, that of doling out unsolicited advice or making comments to strangers on the street concerning their appearance, clothing, or behavior, is completely alien to the American way of thinking. Well-intentioned comments such as "The label is sticking out the back of your sweater," or "You will freeze without a hat," are often not well received by Americans, who perceive such comments as a rude intrusion into their private space rather than as a display of concern, as intended by the Russian. Following her return to Russia after a year of study in the U.S., in answer to a question as to what had struck her most about Americans, one graduate student responded, «Пожалуй, то, что за год никто мне никогда не сделал ни одного поучающего замечания».[88]

Expressions of thanks and gratitude

In English, in most situations to express gratitude a simple—but indispensable—"thank you" will suffice. When talking on the phone or in a hurry, Americans may say "Many thanks." In a situation where a Russian would say «огромное Вам спасибо», the English response could be one of the following phrases: "Thanks so/very much. / Thanks a lot. / Thanks a million. / I'm so grateful to you. / I really appreciate that. / I really appreciate your help/advice. / I won't forget this." ("I won't forget this" may imply that the speaker will be ready to do the other party a favor, or may be planning to reward him in some way, and this meaning of the phrase may not always be obvious to a foreigner.)

In English, "Thank you" is *obligatory* when addressing a salesperson at the end of a transaction, a waiter in a restaurant when he puts the food or the check in front of you, a bank teller who processes your transaction, or a colleague who tells you the time of day. Very often it is specific: "Thank you for your time/trouble/interest."

"Thank you" is used much more often in English than «спасибо» in Russian. Few Russians would thank a sales clerk in a crowded grocery store for returning change or handing over a package; there might be a nod of the head or a kind of "uh-uh" grunt in recognition of the person's services.[89] But since in the U.S. that "thank you" is expected and is nearly always forthcoming, a failure to produce it can be seen as rude.[90]

«Не за что» is usually rendered as "You're welcome," or more formally, "Don't mention it." Some younger speakers replace "you're welcome" with "no problem." In thanking for a particularly large or generous gift the recipient might say, "You really shouldn't have," to which the answer is, "No, no, my pleasure." If the speaker keeps insisting on his gratitude the answer might be, "Really, it's nothing! /Come on! / Don't mention it!", the answer corresponding to the Russian «Ну что Вы»!

In response to a compliment, a simple "thank you" is appropriate. There is no need to try to diminish the value or aesthetic quality of whatever is being praised. For decades in the USSR, however,

Russians were taught a kind of modesty, real or false. This both emphasized the unimportance of an individual as opposed to the collective—"I'm just a small, ordinary person"—and was designed to ward off possible jealousy of others over the acquisition of something of value, as beautiful or expensive items or services were often difficult to obtain during the Soviet era. While a Russian might say «Ну что Вы, эта кофточка совсем старая» or «Да что Вы! Эта прическа мне совсем не к лицу», an American might respond to a compliment with, "Thank you, I got that blouse in Paris last year," or "Thanks, I've been trying out a new hairdresser." In the U.S. there was never any need for false modesty; rather, the tendency has been towards the superlative. The new blouse or hairdo may be "nice," "terrific," "great," "fabulous," "lovely," or some other positive adjective.

Congratulations

Americans are generally less effusive in their congratulations than Russians. For a birthday, a simple "Happy Birthday!" or "I'd like to wish you a very happy birthday" is sufficient. In English you do not «поздравлять» (*congratulate*) someone "with" or "on" a birthday or other holiday, a literal translation of the Russian phrase used for such congratulations. Many adults in the U.S. pay less attention to their birthdays than do Russians, and unless it is a "big one" (круглая дата), they do not feel they have to invite guests to a celebration. And unless they are very close friends, they may not even congratulate adult acquaintances.

The Russian emphasis on birthdays may result both from a conflation of celebrations of a person's saint's day (religious celebrations were banned for years in the USSR) and from the fact that, in a society that constantly emphasized the importance of the collective and the unimportance of the individual, a birthday was the one holiday that clearly belonged solely to the individual and that he/she could celebrate with full impunity. While all that is now part of history, the celebrations of birthdays and their importance to individuals and their families has remained firmly entrenched in Russian culture and tradition.

In English one says "I/We would like to wish you a Merry

Christmas" or just "Merry Christmas!" and "I/We would like to wish you a (very) happy (and healthy) New Year" or just "Happy New Year!" but again, one does not congratulate someone "on" or "with" the holiday.

Excuses and Apologies

In situations requiring an excuse or apology, English once again tends towards brevity: "I'm (so/really) sorry, please excuse me." "Excuse me" is used very frequently, particularly when asking questions of strangers: "Excuse me, would you have the time?" Or, if you've stepped on someone's foot, "Excuse me, I'm (so) sorry."

For a more informal situation, appropriate renderings of colloquial Russian phrases such as «Пустяк!» and «Не велика беда» could be: "It's really nothing!" / "Don't give it another thought." / "Forget about it!" «Это пустяк» and «Все/мало что/ бывает» can be translated as "Forget it," "That's a big nothing" or "That could happen to anyone."

English does not opt for lengthy and flowery apologies. Emotional Russian expressions such as «Как же мне Вам в глаза смотреть?», «Ну и дурак же я!», or «Ой, как же я так всё напутал» sound odd to Americans. An English variation of «Ну дурак же я» will only produce the requisite denials of the individual's stupidity from an American. «Я виноват перед Вами» is rendered as "I owe you an apology," or, if the matter is very serious, "I've done you wrong," but not the literal translation of "I am guilty before you."

The Russian word «претензия», as in «у меня к Вам нет претензий», is often mistranslated as "I have no pretensions/ claims against you." Depending on context, the translation could be: "I'm not blaming you. / I'm not holding you accountable. / I realize you're not to blame. / I realize this is not your fault. / I realize you couldn't do anything about this. / I have nothing against you."

To calm down someone upset over a presumed offense (or anything else), a good translation of «не расстраивайтесь» is "Don't be upset about it" or simply, "Don't worry," or "Don't give it another thought."

The words «обида» and «обидеть» are far more common in Russian than are "offense," "hurt," or "to offend/hurt" in English.

Russian emotions vs. American rationalism, the Russian priority given to moral behavior and personal relations with friends as opposed to business relationships reflect a society in which personal relationships are taken very, very seriously. Versions of «Он меня обидел», «Я на него обижена», or «Ты меня обидишь» are far less frequently heard in English. Since many Americans tend—or at least pretend—to react positively to those around them, there are fewer daily-life situations in which they are likely to announce that they have taken offense or are deeply hurt (aside from those fanatics who are insulted by the slightest deviation from PC language). On the few occasions when an American says, "He offended/insulted me," he is usually referring to a really serious hurt or insult. Otherwise, he is more likely to say "I'm mad/annoyed at him." Where a Russian would say, «Я обижен», the American will say, "I'm upset," rather than "I'm hurt," an expression reserved for serious incidents. For example, "I found out that John threw a big party and didn't invite us, though he's been to our house half a dozen times; I was pretty hurt."

While in Russian frequent use is made of expressions meaning "I am offended," or "He has offended/insulted me," these do not work well in English, and can lead to acquiring a reputation as a difficult, prickly person with whom it is hard to have any sustained professional or personal dealings.

In Russian, «ты меня обидишь» may be used as a mild threat to bring about the desired action on an individual's part when he is being urged or exhorted to do or accept something, e.g. "if you don't come / if you don't accept this present," «ты меня обидишь». More often than not, these magic words will make a Russian yield. This phrase should not be rendered as "you'll insult/offend me," but rather as, "This is for you—I really want you to have this / This is just/especially for you, I'd be really upset if you don't take this." The figurative use of the phrase «Я Вас не обижу», meaning "I'll make this worth your while / I'll pay you well for that" does not work in translation. "I'll be very grateful / I'll take that into account / I won't forget this" conveys that meaning. The expression "not to hurt someone" is idiomatic in Russian contexts but can sound odd in English.

Expressing sympathy and «сочувствие», «соболезнование», regrets, and pity

The words "sympathy/sympathetic" are false friends, for these do not properly translate «симпатия/симпатичный». To "express sympathy" is «выразить сочувствие». "He's in a difficult situation—he has my sympathy," means «Я ему сочувствую».

Russian «симпатия» in English is a "liking" or "fondness" for someone. "I'm sympathetic to your cause" (Отношусь с пониманием к Вашему делу). «Он очень симпатичный человек» means that "He's a very nice/sweet/pleasant person."

In English, expressing "sympathy" or "deepest sympathy" is the standard form for written condolences on someone's death. (A Russian émigré who wanted to express her gratitude to a man who had been very helpful to her in trying to find a job sent him a greeting card with the inscription "Thank you for your sympathy." The astonished American gently told her that such cards were sent by family members to thank those who had expressed their «соболезнования по случаю кончины близкого человека».) An appropriate oral expression of condolences on someone's death is «Примите мои соболезнования», "I'm so sorry (about your sister)" or "I was so sorry to hear about your sister."

The behavior of Russians and Americans at a time of intense grief, such as at a funeral, also differs. An American widow who does not cry at her husband's funeral and does not verbally and nonverbally show excessive emotion will be praised by her friends and relatives for "showing such control and restraint." A Russian woman who showed no strong and visible emotions at her husband's funeral, however, would be viewed by her family and friends as cold and probably not very attached to her deceased spouse.

The word "sorry" can also be used to render both an expression of sympathy and the concept of feeling sorry in general, «жалеть». "I am/feel sorry for him" means «Мне его жалко / я его жалею». In Russian, however, «жалеть» is used more often than the equivalent expression in English, "to feel sorry for" someone. Some prefer the phrase "I really feel for him," closer to the meaning of «Я ему сочувствую».

More often than not, «жаль/жалко/жалею» does not mean "It's a pity" or "I pity him." «Мне его жалко—больная жена, трое маленьких детей» can be translated as "I'm sorry for him / He has my sympathy / I sympathize with him / That's really terrible for him / I feel for him," but not as "I pity him." To pity is an extremely strong verb, emphasizing the gap (often one of condescension) between the speaker and the addressee. It can imply a patronizing attitude to a person in trouble, or indicate that he may be partially to blame for his unfortunate situation: "I really pity him—he didn't study all semester, now he's flunked out of school, and has nowhere to go." In Russian the meaning may be much milder, hence the fairly common abuse of "pity" by Russian speakers.

On the other hand, the expression "It's a pity that …" can be a reasonable translation of «Очень жаль». "It's a pity / It's too bad … we didn't know you were in New York—we could have all gone out together."

> Я жалею, что Вы не пришли на наш прием.
> *I'm sorry you couldn't come to our party/reception.*

> Очень жаль/жалко/что так все вышло—хотелось бы поговорить!
> *Too bad that happened / It's a shame that happened—I really would have liked to talk/chat with you.*

In formal speech, "regret" is an appropriate translation of «жалеть»:

> Мы жалеем о том, что не включили поправки к документу.
> *We regret that we didn't include the amendments to this document.*

Another expression equivalent to «Очень жаль» in English—and which frequently confuses Russian speakers—is "It's a shame that …" But there is no implication here of «стыдно» or «постыдно, что», that anything is "shameful." The meaning is purely "It's too bad that / I regret that / I am sorry that," e.g. "It's a shame I didn't know he was looking for a job—there was an opening in our firm which would have been perfect for him."

Как «мыть руки» (How to "wash your hands")

One of the most embarrassing moments in any foreign culture is the search for toilet facilities. Russians can go wrong by not realizing that in most American apartments and houses the toilet and sink are in the same room as the bathtub, and that the word "bathroom" therefore includes the toilet. In public places these facilities are called "rest rooms," a word that sounds like a lounge to the Russian ear. While in Russia it is not quite acceptable to ask a person of the opposite sex (a waiter, usher, gas station attendant) for the location of these facilities, in America this is considered perfectly normal.

I'm right — You're wrong

One of the biggest problems for Russians speaking English in America is what can be called the question of dogmatism. Without the slightest intention of doing so, Russians occasionally antagonize Americans with what sound like dogmatic, extremely self-confident statements. The two languages and cultures differ radically in accepted ways of voicing differences of opinion and regarding the fundamental concepts of what is "right" (правильный) and "wrong" (неправильный)—and how to express them.

Suppose that an American declares that, "Russians and Americans are exactly alike. They're open, honest, friendly, live in huge nations, love their countries." Another American strongly disagrees—he thinks that Russians and Americans are very different. What does he say to the first speaker? If a Russian were to say, «Вы неправы», that would not in the least upset his fellow-countrymen. An American, however, will almost never say, "You're wrong," as it is considered highly discourteous. For decades the doctrinaire ways of Marxist ideology were so deeply etched into the minds of the Soviet population that few people—even those who consciously rejected the system—failed to be affected by the authoritarian Soviet mindset. The result was habitual thinking in terms of either "right" (правильно) or "wrong," (неправильно) with no gray areas in between.[91]

Most Americans tend to reject the notion that philosophical systems can explain everything, and that there is always a "right" or a "wrong" answer. Several options should be explored and the best choice made. Agreement can be voiced by: "I think so, too. / I think that is so. / I support your view." From elementary school on, Americans are trained to preface their views with phrases like "In my opinion," "It's possible you may be right, but," or "This could be viewed another way, too." «Правильный» is used in several specific situations:

> Он неправильно написал ее фамилию.
> *He misspelled her name.*

> Совершенно правильно, что его выбрали
> председателем этого комитета.
> *It was absolutely appropriate that he was elected*
> *chairman of the committee.*

Unless we are talking about something purely technical, such as how to operate a piece of machinery, the notion that there is a «правильный» (*right*) or «неправильный» (*wrong*) way of doing things drives Americans crazy. There's your way and there's my way. From the American standpoint, you have your point of view and I have mine—not "I am right" and "you are wrong." And who are you—or I—to say which one is «правильный». You like vanilla, and I like chocolate. This is your way and this is my way, and here lies a fundamental difference between languages and cultures.

In voicing views and opinions, however, Russians tend to be highly categorical, using assertions such as: «Вы не правы», «Это неправда», and «Это не так». These "loaded" phrases are perfectly acceptable in Russian discourse, while in the U.S., unless you are talking about something inherently correct like the sum of two and two or the spelling of a word, no answer is considered "right" or "correct." Implying that you know the "correct" answer in an argument is badly received in a society where relativism is king. The equally common Russian phrase «Это неправда» (*This is ... not true / an untruth / wrong*) is a highly emotionally charged assertion that the other person is not only wrong but also—and perhaps deliberately—distorting the truth, and it will come across as quite offensive in English.

Literal translation of Russian words with the root «коррект-» can cause offense. If something needs «корректировка», or if there is a need to «корректировать», in English this may need to be "adapted/adjusted/changed," not "corrected." «Некорректное поведение» in English translation is "inappropriate" or "improper," not "incorrect" or "wrong" behavior.

Even though in their use of language Americans tend to be "active" rather than "passive," the reverse is true regarding the expression of personal opinion. There may be use of some active phrases such as "I think that," or "I'd suggest that," or "We might try another approach," but here American English tends to prefer passive and impersonal constructions: "It seems to me that / In my opinion / There might be / One might think that / It could (also) be said that," etc. Such forms of stating views show that the speaker is being polite and courteous. For a Russian, however, these phrases make the speaker sound unsure of himself or hesitant; to a Russian a view should be expressed politely but firmly.

Failure to take this basic distinction in attitudes into account can spoil relationships between Russians and Americans. A simple "I'd look at it this way" or "I don't quite agree with that" will always work. Of course, if someone is suggesting something morally outrageous—"All disabled people should be shot"—you can say, "No, I can't agree with that" or "No, I can't go along with that," or "No, I'd find that (absolutely) unacceptable." As a Russian observer of the American scene noted, «В американской культуре приветствуется бесконфликтное общение ... Не принято возражать гостям, и тем более спорить с ними. Если возникает атмосфера несогласия, то обычно вежливо констатируется расхождение во взглядах и разговор переводится на другую тему».[92]

In the U.S. a serious, knockdown argument among friends is rare indeed. Arguing and debating are not considered as basically pleasurable or as a sport. The American style of debate and argumentation is not aggressive or confrontational; a disagreement is something to be resolved by various means, including compromise. Respect, and the voicing of that respect, for the other person's opinion is a *sine qua non*: "We agree to disagree" or "Let's agree to disagree," notions that are virtually untranslatable and incomprehensible to Russians. A favorite and common phrase in Russian is «Я категорически несогласен» (*I categorically/absolutely/totally disagree*), a phrase not popular in American English, as the emphasis is usually on highlighting agreement and similarity rather than disagreement. In Russian the word «толерантность» is a relatively new addition to the language, whereas "tolerance" has long been basic to the American mentality.[93]

The common Russian expression «Это факт», if translated as "This is a fact," is likely to antagonize Americans. Most of the time the speaker is merely asserting the conviction that his assumption is backed by some kind of evidence such as various published materials. "I think that's been proven/shown," or "There is a lot of evidence/materials to support/back that" are more tactful ways of putting this in English.

The literal translation of the Russian phrase «Я это знаю точно» (*I know this exactly*) when making the assertion that something is true, is very off-putting to Americans. The idea is "I'm (quite) sure of that / I know that for sure."

Unless a speaker is taking the floor in a formal meeting, «Я не возражаю» should not be translated as "I do not object" or "I have no objections." In normal conversation the English rendering would be "I can accept that" or "I'll go along with that" or "I can agree with that."

Вы не возражаете против того, чтобы закрыть окно?
Do you mind closing / Could I bother you to close ...
the window?

Он не возражает, если я приду чуть-чуть раньше?
Would he mind / Would it be okay with him / Would
it be all right with him ... if I came a little earlier?

A good translation for «Не может быть!» rather than "That's impossible!" could be "You don't say!" or "You must be kidding/joking," or "Come on!" In English an objection is often prefaced by "I would say, however, that … (there are other factors at work here / data have shown different results)" or "It could perhaps be said that (more work remains to be done here / this is not the only solution)". For English speakers these modals, "would, could, should" which do not have direct equivalents in Russian, make a world of difference. "I would suggest that we should take his views into account" is a polite-sounding statement, while "We must take his views into account" can raise the listeners' hackles. A negative interrogative with a modal verb form also "softens" the speaker's objection or argument, e.g.: "Couldn't we agree that … / Wouldn't it be a good idea if … / Might it not be good to …"

Another "dogmatic softener" is "I'm afraid that"—e.g., "I'm afraid that if we follow your argument to its logical conclusion, we'll be preaching fanaticism." Such phrases as, "I hope you don't mind if I'm perfectly frank in saying … / Frankly … / To be perfectly honest/candid I think that … / Wouldn't it be better to say … / I was wondering whether …" also tone down the categorical nature of the speaker's assertion.[94]

Some constructions that sound perfectly "normal" to Russian speakers if translated literally into English can reinforce the impression of dogmatic and categorical thinking, or of "thinking negative." As discussed previously, words and expressions like «нельзя», «не надо», and «не нужно», present precisely such a negative image to Americans. In literal translation, this negative and categorical sense is intensified: "One must not / It is not possible / It is not convenient" create a dogmatic as well as a negative picture of the language and culture, leftovers of the Soviet culture of bans, of what is forbidden by the authorities, and the risk of penalties for violating these restrictions.

The Russian speaker may also sound categorical when using "positive" forms of impersonal constructions, even when that is definitely not his intention. For example, «Надо пойти в магазин/закончить эту работу», rendered literally is "It is necessary to go to the store" / "It is necessary to finish this work." The constructions "There is a need to do this" or "There is a need to take measures to stop this" would be fine for formal prose, but not for informal conversation. Here a personal pronoun can be used with a verb such as "need to / have to / got to" to soften the sentence: "I/We have (got) to go to the store / We need to go to the store / I/We have (got) to finish this job." Using "must," as in, "I must go to the store" implies an urgent and immediate need to perform the action, more urgent than what the speaker intended to say in Russian.

> Надо много работать на этой неделе.
> *I/We have to work hard this week. / I've/We've got a lot of work to do this week. / This will be a rough week.*

A final comment on debates, arguments, and disagreements. Americans generally do not raise their voices during a discussion. Arguments, discussions, and conversations consist of back and forth repartee, a kind of verbal ping-pong, not a series of monologues. Gently interrupting an interlocutor shows that the speaker is in fact following what the person is saying. Of course, everyone has a right to state an opinion without being interrupted every second. But a "monologue" or statement lasting more than a few minutes is often considered by Americans as rude, depriving others of the right to speak, and will open the way to interruptions. "Keep it short" is the motto in the U.S. And we can never forget the importance of time for Americans, even time spent debating highly interesting subjects.

6.

The Time Is Out of Joint

~

Attitudes towards time are fundamental to human behavior. The concept of time and the words used to define time units differ radically in many languages, including Russian and English. Though technically a minute consists of the same 60 seconds, the meaning of "just a minute" is quite different in Russia and America.

Defining time as monochronic and polychronic, the American anthropologist Edward Hall created one of the best known theoretical frameworks for examining various cultures' concepts of time.[95] In a monochronic (also known as fixed-time) culture such as the U.S. (England, Germany, and the Scandinavian cultures share this orientation) time is perceived as a frame for behavior. In the past, an American would focus his entire attention on one event before turning to the next one. Now, even though "multi-tasking" has taken over, the basic focus is still on the specific task or tasks to be performed rather than on the relationships of the people involved. An American takes deadlines very seriously, values efficiency, and attaches great importance to short-term as well as long-standing relationships, be they with a person with whom he is concluding a one-time business deal and may never see again, or a long-time tennis partner.

For Russian culture (as well as for many Mediterranean, Arab, Latin American, and some Asian cultures), time is basically polychronic. Attention is focused simultaneously on several events, and the individual tends to be quite flexible regarding his planned activities.[96] In these cultures greater importance is attached to long-term relationships than to short-term relationships, and a schedule is readily changed on the request of a friend or relative. Relationship needs rather than time demands often determine when something will be started or completed, and these frequently take precedence over business relationships.

Today in the corporate world of both America and Russia, meetings start on time. A ten o'clock appointment means ten o'clock, and the visitor is well advised to be there at five to ten, not at ten-fifteen. If someone is late, explanations such as "the traffic was awful" will not cut much ice. An American believes in leaving early enough to allow for traffic jams or other such eventualities.

In the U.S. fixed-time culture spills over from the business sphere into other areas. A lecture or dinner party will start at the indicated time. An American is not happy when his friend has arrived an hour late, and may be angry at him for having wasted so much time. In fact, for some Americans, time is more important than relationships or friendships. And an American is less likely than the Russian to find an excuse for his friend's lateness, such as, "Well, he lives so far" or "He's having such a difficult time at home."

In the U.S. people plan ahead. An invitation to lunch three weeks from now is perfectly normal, for the American feels that he controls time and the course of events, and not the other way round. He specifies the date, place and exact time: "On May 22, three weeks from Tuesday, at the French restaurant Chez Jean on the southwest corner of 35th Street and Third Avenue, at 1:15." There is no need to «созвониться» (*call each other*) the day before the meeting to confirm. Since the American wants to know exactly when he has an appointment, he finds the vagueness of «созвониться», which does not have a direct equivalent in English, quite puzzling. Does «мы созвонимся» mean that you will call me or that I will call you? The verb can be rendered in English as "We'll call each other," or "We'll be in touch." For an American the suggestion that the other party call back to confirm the lunch may be taken as an indication that the individual doubts he will be able to—or actually wants to—make this meeting. If there is really a need to call to check whether the date is still on, the closest polite equivalent is "I'll call you the day before just in case anything unexpected comes up." Russians tend to feel that "who knows what might happen three weeks from now." Three weeks ahead?

Who knows what «судьба» (*fate*) may have in store that far in the future? Anything could happen; no one can predict or direct the course of events. The American, on the other hand, thinks that (or would like to believe that) since he has control of events the future is foreseeable and predictable. Since he is concentrating on the present and a carefully planned future, long-term planning is very important. An American journalist noted the popularity in English of words with the prefix "pre-" meaning "in advance": "precooked meals," "prewashed denim," "preboarding" at the airport gate.[97] The difference between the American and Russian attitude towards advance planning is nicely illustrated by an incident recounted by a Russian writer living in the West:

> Звонит нам одна знакомая, приглашает на борщ. Специально для нас она сварит настоящий русский борщ. Когда? Ну, скажем, в ближайшее воскресенье. Нет, в воскресенье мы не можем, в воскресенье мы заняты. Тогда в следующее воскресенье? И в следующее … Тогда еще через неделю? Ну, что ты будешь делать? Так я и записала себе в календарь: борщ, знакомая, через три недели.
>
> Ну разве может быть такое в Москве? Сварила я борщ, или приехал кто-то, или книгу интересную принес, или прости гениальная мысль пришла—неужели я буду ждать три недели? Сейчас! Немедленно! Бросай всё! И приходи! И приходили …[98]

There is a serious point to this story. For Americans, it is important to treat both one's own time and that of other people with the greatest respect. Inviting someone to come over at the last minute is disrespectful because it implies that the person's time is not important, that he has no plans of his own and can come over whenever you decide you want him around. The same holds true for dropping in without an invitation.[99] Because it shows a total disregard for the other person's schedule, «на огонек» is considered by Americans as the height of rudeness. (Not surprisingly, there is no idiomatic English equivalent for this custom, which is becoming increasingly less common in today's westernized Russia.)

Like money, time used positively is "spent, " "saved," "gained," "filled," "made the most of." In Russian, however, «мы проводим», not «тратим время». In English, time used carelessly is "lost," "wasted," or "squandered." Unplanned time can even be " killed," e.g., "I arrived so early for my doctor's appointment that I had to kill half an hour window-shopping."[100] It is to "save time" that lunch in America may be planned three months ahead and that so much business is conducted over "power breakfasts" (a breakfast at which major deals may be discussed or concluded) and business lunches and dinners. As the American saying goes, "There's no such thing as a free lunch" (Бесплатный сыр бывает только в мышеловке). Everything has a price, and the person who invites you to lunch is probably assuming that the results of the meal's business conversation will justify its cost. The expression "quality time" has become increasingly popular. Spending "quality time" with a client—or with your children—means that you are actively involved every minute, not sitting around or focusing your attention on someone or something else, or, if you are multitasking, on several people or things.

Americans do not forgive those who waste their time through a lack of punctuality or carelessness in keeping appointments. Even though today in Russia there have been enormous changes in attitudes towards time, and the younger generation of business people is as aware as Americans of the importance of punctuality, traces of the old mentality still make themselves felt. In Soviet post-Stalinist times being late for work did not result in major disciplinary action. As one Russian commentator noted, «К сожалению, русские довольно беспечно и вольно обращаются не только со своим, но и с чужим временем. Вы должны простить нашу необязательность и непунктуальность.»[101] As many Russians have discovered, however, Americans are loath to do so.

Time is so highly quantified in America precisely *because* it equals money. When an American tells a friend he will meet him in ten minutes he usually means exactly that—ten, and not twenty. If he says he will finish a project in five months, he will do so, requesting an extension only if something truly drastic has occurred, not by invoking vague "health" or "family" reasons.

America has a fixed concept of time, while Russian time is fluid. "Fixed-time cultures" perceive time in terms of precisely defined units. For Americans, a minute is literally sixty seconds. When an American says "I'll be with you in a minute" he means just that— two or three minutes at most. To the dismay of the American, a Russian «минуточку» or «сию минуту» can easily run to ten or fifteen minutes.

Another confusing "time word" is «момент». Not all the meanings of this polysemic Russian word are covered by the English word "moment." One Russian meaning of the word is that of a very brief period or point in time, similar to the sense of the English word "moment." Saying "Just a moment" in Russian is fine; in English, however, the word "please" must be added to avoid sounding rude. "Excuse me, I'll be there in just a minute," or "Excuse me, I'll be through in just a minute" is fine. «Момент —сейчас приду» can be rendered as "I'll be there in a minute." "He'll be with you in just a few moments" is a virtual synonym of "in a few minutes." "Would you have a moment now?" means "Would you have a few minutes?" The word can also indicate an appropriate time: "This is not the right moment to talk to him about that matter."

The Russian «момент» also means a feature/aspect/component/ element of a matter, a nuance that cannot be rendered by the English "moment." «Положительный/важный момент» can be a positive element or feature of a report, statement, or project. «Нам нужно учесть этот момент» means "We must take this aspect/point/issue into account." Or «важный момент в жизни человека» can be an important period/event/stage/turning point in someone's life. A «принципиальный момент» is an important point/element/ aspect, but has nothing to do with "principal" or "principles," and is never a "moment." To an English speaker the statement "You do not understand this moment" sounds very strange, though there are some instances where "moment" works, such as "A very special moment" or "I'll remember this moment forever."

"Right away" in American English means *just that*. «Сейчас» in Russian is a highly fluid concept, covering a time period ranging anywhere from five to twenty-five minutes. To an American "right away" (сейчас) does not mean, "Yes, I'll be with you when I've finished what I'm doing now," but literally "right now, this minute." In English "I'm coming," or "I'll be there" conveys the sense that something will be done very soon, though not necessarily within the next five minutes.

The expression «в ближайшем будущем» is another cause of miscommunication. "I'll do it in the very near future" does not convey the notion that something will be done soon but not "right this minute." A stricter definition of "time when" is needed, such as "I'll do it … in the next few days / this week / in the next two weeks." "Very soon" is also less binding on the speaker. The word «оперативно» is a "false friend" of the translator, for «Будет сделано оперативно» means that something will be done quickly/promptly/effectively/efficiently.

Russian expressions indicating "time when" can seem maddeningly vague to Americans. In literal translation, «Я позвоню Вам завтра во второй половине дня» conveys no information. To a Russian this means some time after noon, while to an American it means sometime after 2 pm. "I'll call you tomorrow afternoon" would be much clearer, and a more specific answer such as "I'll phone you tomorrow between three and four" is better still.

Similarly, statements such as «Он будет к трем часам» or «Приходите к семи» are also confusing if translated literally. Americans would say, "He'll be back by three," or, if that is not a total certainty, "He should be back by three."

While in both Russia and America punctuality is the accepted norm for business dealings, there are differences in time perception in regard to social gatherings. When inviting guests for dinner, an American will ask his friends to "come at seven," but not "around seven." And "seven" means guests are expected to arrive at seven or at the latest by seven-fifteen, not at seven-thirty. If a guest is going to be late because of heavy traffic or an emergency, a phone call is in order.

Since Americans are sure that the hostess will be ready to receive her guests at the time when she has invited them, they are not doing her any favors by being late. That may only help wreck the dinner, now burning away in the oven. The Russian hostess, however, is very often counting on that extra time to finish her preparations.

An invitation to an American, «приходите к нам к шести/часов в шесть» needs to be rendered in English with greater precision. Does that mean at 6:00? At 6:15? The American would like to know for sure. «Давайте встретимся около трех» presents the same kind of problem. "Let's meet at 2:45" would make things clear.

It is also difficult to correctly render in English the common time expression «уже седьмой час», which can mean anything from 6:01 to 6:59. There is no direct English equivalent for this construction. "It's already well after/past six" would convey the meaning.

For Americans the day is divided into "in the morning" (from roughly nine until noon), "lunchtime" (from about noon until two), "in the afternoon" (from two to five), and "in the evening" (from about six to ten). Care should be taken in rendering «после обеда» into English. It should be made clear that «обед» here means "lunch" (for which the Russian word «ланч» now provides a crystal-clear equivalent) and not "dinner." Americans tend to interpret «после обеда» as meaning right after lunch, and not "during the afternoon." (An American couple living in Moscow who had hired a Russian няня for their four-year-old son were nonplussed when she told them one evening of her concern because «после обеда Джонни ничего не ел». This made no sense to the parents. If he had been served a reasonable amount of food, why should the kid eat something right after lunch?)

Usage differs regarding the adjective «вечерний». To a Russian «вечернее заседание» or «вечерняя сессия» may mean a meeting held some time after lunch, i.e., in the afternoon. In English an "evening meeting" takes place after six in the evening. «Два часа ночи» is usually "two o'clock in the morning," sometimes "two o'clock at night." Time is often indicated by the abbreviations "AM" (from midnight until noon) and "PM" covering noon until midnight. Thus "2:00 PM" refers to two in the afternoon, while "2:00 AM" is two o'clock at night (or in the morning). Many Americans are unfamiliar with the European system using 13:00-24:00 for the time from 1:00 PM to midnight (it is only used in the military in the U.S.). Saying, "This play starts at 19:30" can mean that an American friend will never get there.[102]

Mistakes are often made by English-speaking Russians when referring to «вчера вечером», «сегодня вечером», and «завтра вечером». These must be translated as "last night," "this evening," and "tomorrow evening/night," never as "tomorrow in the night." «Вчера ночью меня разбудил шум на улице» is "Last night I was awakened by noise in the street," never "Yesterday in the night …" «Сегодня утром» is "*this* morning," and «сегодня днем» is "*this* afternoon." The word "today" is not used in these expressions, and the literal translation "today in the morning" does not work in English. «Вчера утром» is "yesterday morning" and «вчера днем» is "yesterday afternoon." «Завтра утром» is "tomorrow morning," and «завтра днем» is "tomorrow afternoon." «Я тебя встречу завтра в два часа дня» is "I'll meet you at two tomorrow afternoon," not "at two of the afternoon."

Another confusing time expression is the Janus-faced «на днях», which can mean either "within the *last* few days" (на днях я об этом узнала), or "within the *next* few days" (Я на днях Вам дам ответ). In English this phrase must be time-specific: "I found out … only just *a few days ago / very recently*." To indicate that it is future-oriented, «на днях» can be rendered by "I'll get back to you with/about/concerning that issue … *within the next few days / in a couple of days / in a day or two*." «На выходные» translates as "on weekends," e.g., "On weekends they go to their country house," and "During the weekend they like to play golf."

Respect for time also applies to telephone behavior. When calling on business, the American will spend only a few minutes on an exchange of social niceties and then immediately get down to business. Even starting off a business conversation with a specific request or with "What can I do for you?" is quite acceptable. In Russia, the telephone is on a pedestal. If a friend calls while dinner is getting cold, the guests are at the door, or the plane is about to leave—all that can wait at least for a little while. But if someone telephones while an American is having dinner, he will most likely say, "I'd really like to talk to you, but we just sat down to dinner.

Could I call you back in an hour?" Or, if guests have just arrived, "I'd love to chat with you, but I have company/guests/people here. … When could I get back to you? / What would be a good time to call you? / Will you be home later/tomorrow?"

Another way of showing respect for a person's time and schedule—and that is very much in the interest of the person making the phone call—is to begin by saying, "Hello, John, this is Igor. Is this a good time for you?" (Вам удобно говорить?) This does not always occur to Russians who often feel that a phone takes precedence over other activities. And it is advisable for an American to ask a Russian if this is a good time for him to talk, since he may not be forthcoming about the fact that this is in fact a rather inconvenient time for him, with negative results for the ensuing conversation.

In addition to the differences between monochronic vs. diachronic, or fixed vs. fluid categories of time, a third kind of temporal distinction occurs between past-oriented and present-future-oriented cultures. "Time waits for no man" is a favorite American saying. "Take care of today and tomorrow will take care of itself" is another.[103] And attitudes toward time affect how people speak. Living in the present means being practical, direct, informal, and above all—in the interest of saving time and money—succinct and to the point. Subtlety, irony, and hidden meanings are not ingrained in American speech. People in the U.S. tend to speak directly and to the point, and to call a spade a spade. When Americans leave a group or a party, they do not always say good-bye to each person individually, and often they save time by saying one farewell to the whole group or to two or three groups of people. No one would be insulted «тем, что он со мной не попрощался». Indeed, some Americans might find it odd for someone to "make the rounds" by taking leave of everyone.

The American conversational style differs radically from that of most Russians. For Americans simplicity and brevity are the soul of wit and wisdom, and Americans find the endless Russian stories and monologues that dominate so many Russian get-togethers boring and artificial. Russians, on the other hand, may find the American style of short answers and the ping-pong of repartee brusque and rude. When answering a question, Americans get straight to the point. "When my mother asked my Russian husband how his aunt was doing," complained one young American woman, "he came back with her entire biography." While a Russian feels it is discourteous to give a short answer, and that complex ideas require time in order for the formulation of thoughtful responses, an American resents being held captive to a lengthy monologue.

As the anthropologist Edward Hall noted, Americans believe in being direct. "Most Americans keep their social conversations light, rather than engaging in serious, intellectual or philosophical discussions, a trait which especially bothers Europeans."[104] These kinds of differences in language style have caused difficulty in intercultural communication on the highest level. The well-known American psycholinguist Deborah Tannen wrote that:

> I would wager that the much-publicized antipathy
> between Nancy Reagan and Raisa Gorbachev
> resulted from cultural differences in conversational
> style. According to Nancy Reagan, "From the
> moment we met she talked and talked and *talked*
> —so much that I could barely get a word in,
> edgewise or otherwise." I suspect that if anyone had
> asked Raissa Gorbachev, she would say that she'd
> been wondering why her American counterpart
> never said anything and made her do all the
> conversational work.[105]

Barbara Bush spoke to the same subject when she described her conversation with Raisa Gorbacheva, who asked her why Nancy Reagan had taken a dislike to her. Mrs. Bush noted that the Russian president's wife essentially answered her own question when she commented that she was unfamiliar with American customs. Though she dominated the entire conversation, she undoubtedly thought this was what was expected of her.[106] The linguistic-cultural differences are quite clear. Raisa Maximovna felt that it was her duty to "entertain" Mrs. Reagan, who was irritated by the series of lengthy monologues. And the same kind of communication failure occurs daily in contacts between ordinary Russians and Americans.

7.

The Art of Eating

~

No one can live without eating. Sharing food and meals for social and business purposes, on joyous and sad occasions, is common to all cultures, though in very different forms. In America people have long gotten together for breakfast, lunch, and dinner for business purposes as well as for family and social reasons. Behavior while sharing food sometimes differs greatly and sometimes differs in small but important ways from culture to culture. Certain Russian and American habits are strikingly different.

First a few notes on basic vocabulary. In English, what we eat is "food," what stores sell is "food," and the industry that produces it is the "food products" industry. There are certain foods grown and eaten in a particular place or country, e.g. "the foods of Spain." The way these foods are prepared is the kind of "cooking" (кухня) of the country; a cookbook could be entitled "Spanish Cooking." A more elegant word for the way a nation or people prepare food is "cuisine," i.e., the elegance of "French cuisine." "Kitchen," the English literal translation of the Russian word «кухня», only means the room in which food is prepared, and does not have any figurative meanings; you do not talk about a "French kitchen" or a "political kitchen." A «блюдо» is a "dish," as in "hot dishes," "cold dishes," "someone's favorite dish."

The commonly used English word "meal" does not exist in Russian. The closest equivalent to this notion of food eaten at any time of day, be it breakfast, lunch, or dinner, is the slightly archaic-sounding «трапеза». "I'd like to have you over for a meal" does not have a specific meaning in Russian, aside from an invitation to share food and company at someone's home, probably at lunch or dinner; an American will always specify the precise time of day for his invitation.

Breakfast, Lunch, and Dinner

For Americans the first meal of the day is "breakfast," and a "power breakfast" (so far not popular in Russia) is yet one more convenient time-saving activity for people who may begin the day in a fairly expensive restaurant (often located in a hotel) to discuss business with their associates and guests. Needless to say, food is secondary to the conversation and this is rarely a leisurely occasion. For a "business meal" there are significant cultural differences between Russians and Americans. At a business meal, be it breakfast, lunch, or dinner, Americans do not first gulp down the food and then talk business; the functions of eating and talking are carried on simultaneously. Nowadays Russians have become used to this practice of "talking while eating," though the older generation of Russians is still accustomed to first eating, while engaging in primarily social conversation, and only then turning to business discussions. This can be strange for the American host who does not understand why the Russian is wasting so much of the "business meal" chitchatting.

In America lunch, now known in Russian as «ланч», can be eaten anytime between 12:00 and 2:00. «Ланч» is ripe with possibilities for gastronomic, linguistic, and cultural confusion. In Russia the meal eaten at midday is also called «обед», usually translated in English as "dinner." But at 12:00 noon an American does not say "I'm going to have dinner," but "I'm going to have lunch."

As opposed to the Russian «обед», which is usually considered the larger main meal of the day, for an American the noontime meal often consists of a sandwich or salad. It does not necessarily include a soup, meat, or any other hot dish. A Russian who is invited for lunch is unlikely to content himself with a soup and sandwich. While a business lunch in a restaurant may be a three-course meal, Americans usually eat their main meal in the evening.

An invitation to an American home for "dinner" generally means an evening meal some time between six and eight o'clock in the evening. Guests are expected to arrive within 15 minutes of the time indicated by the host, not later, as is often the case in Russia. Buffet dinners, which allow for more flexibility in terms of the time for the guests' arrival, are quite rare in Russia.

In the U.S. an invitation to have "a cup of coffee" or "a cup of tea" means exactly that. This is in no way equivalent to the hospitality and «угощение» understood in the Russian invitation «приходите к нам на чай» (*Come over for a cup of tea*). The American host will literally serve a cup of coffee or tea, and perhaps a few cookies or a slice of cake. There is no expectation that there will be any other kind of food or drink or the kinds of "zakuski," salads, or other dishes served in Russia. Over and over, Americans invited to Russian homes for "a cup of tea" have been surprised to find an entire meal on the table, often with a variety of appetizers and desserts. Russians are therefore often taken aback to discover that if someone suggests "going out for coffee," this means going to a café and at most ordering a piece of pie or a cookie along with the coffee. And an invitation to an American's house at an hour that does not coincide with lunch or dinner time does not by any means indicate that a meal will be served. It would be unthinkable to have a guest in a Russian home, regardless of the time of day, without ample food on the table.

At the table

Americans are occasionally surprised when Russians start eating before everyone has been served, or before the hostess has begun to eat; in Russia this is quite acceptable behavior. True, sometimes the American hostess will say, "Please start / Don't wait for me … or the food will get cold," which nicely resolves that question.

If a dinner party is going well and conversation is flowing, Russians may not start moving towards the door as early as Americans, particularly on weekdays. Nor will Russians necessarily call to thank the next day, though many by now have begun to do so.

Cocktails, Anyone?

The "cocktail hour" from about 5 to 7 o'clock in the evening is a new experience for many Russians. While vodka-drinking bouts are legendary, and many Russians nowadays are getting used to wine, in Russia alcoholic drinks are always served *with* a meal, not *before* it, and cocktail parties are not usual occurrences. Drinking with no food or minimal food seems very odd to most Russians, and with good reason. Since food (particularly buttered bread) absorbs a good deal of alcohol, serious drinking is best done with food! But the notion of "drinking at the table" with no "pre-dinner" drinks seems strange to Americans.

At home many Americans have a drink before dinner in the evenings, and guests are *always* offered a pre-dinner drink, which a Russian may find unusual. This usually takes the form of the question, "What can I get you? " or "What would you like?"— i.e. "What can I get you to drink?" Russians are often surprised that there may be very little food to accompany these drinks, perhaps only some cheese and crackers, or raw vegetables with dips. Nor should the American host assume that the Russian will understand the question "straight up, or on the rocks?" "Mixed drinks," made with soda water or tonic water, are not very common in Russia.

The overwhelming majority of American hosts never exert any pressure to have an alcoholic drink, and some Russians may not be aware that, if someone does not drink at all, the simple sentence "I don't drink" is quite sufficient. Whether a guest has an upset stomach, is a recovering alcoholic, a Mormon, or simply dislikes the taste of alcohol is of no interest to anyone, and a lengthy explanation is not necessary. The term "soft drink" may also need an explanation, as in Russian these are sometimes referred to as "some kind of water." And in the U.S. "lemonade" is a combination of water, sugar, and lemon juice, usually served in summer, that has nothing to do with the Russian «лимонад», a fizzy kind of sweetened fruit soda.

Socializing at a cocktail party in the U.S. and at Russian gatherings operate on very different premises, and cocktail parties are not common in Russia, though recently they have started to become fashionable in certain circles. Since the purpose of the cocktail party is to have people "mingle" (общаться), they are supposed to talk to as many other people as possible, and to keep moving, spending only a short period of time with each individual. An American host may perform a few introductions, but otherwise no particular effort is made to introduce the guests to each other. People are often chosen precisely because they *don't* know each other and the host thinks it would be interesting for them to meet. It is up to the guests to take the initiative in starting conversations both with people they know and with strangers. In Russia, however, the assumption at most gatherings is that at least a few of the people present do know each other, and those who do not are unlikely to take the initiative in making acquaintance with strangers.

It is quite customary at an American cocktail party for people to walk up to individuals they do not know and introduce themselves: "Hello, I'm John Stone." Usually this is followed by something placing the individual in context, e.g.: "I work with David (the host)" or "I'm Jane's (the hostess) aunt." Ways of beginning a conversation with these unknown individuals (the weather is used only in desperation) include: "That's a lovely painting on the wall" / "How long have you known David? / Where do you know David from?" To move to get away from a bore or a pest or simply when you are done your conversation, a remark such as "Well, I'll go get a refill (of my drink)", or simply, "Nice to talk to you," is appropriate and will not be considered rude. On the contrary, sticking to the same person for a very long time at a cocktail party is a kind of violation of the "get out and meet people" rule. This runs directly counter to Russian rules of socializing, for people will rarely supply such background information about themselves, and talking very briefly to someone and moving on is perceived as quite rude behavior.

The American attitude towards drinking at parties and dinners differs radically from that of Russians. No matter how much a person has drunk, in the U.S. he will be held responsible for everything he says, with no indulgence for lapses in taste or behavior. If a guest has made negative or tactless comments about individuals or ethnic groups, argued loudly and aggressively, or stumbled while getting up, no one will say with an understanding smile, «Ну, он же был подвыпившим». He will simply be considered a crude boor, and will never receive another invitation from the hosts. So, drinker beware.

Americans are also fond of buffets (шведский стол). (The Russian cognate «буфет» has a different meaning.) Cocktail parties and buffets are particularly popular in the U.S. because, as opposed to Russians, Americans do not like being "stuck" at a table, sitting next to the same people all evening, and both the cocktail party and the buffet provide constant opportunities for moving around. Since serious conversations are not very common at such gatherings—as they are in Russia with a group seated around one big table—this also ensures that no truly substantive discussions will take place.

At cocktails or buffets, aside from the host saying, "help yourself" when a guest comes in, there is no effort to ply people with food or drink. The "do-it-yourself" approach reigns here. (A Russian host or hostess, however, is constantly offering more food and drink.) When Americans say, "help yourself" they mean it, and when a host says to a house guest, "Help yourself to whatever is in the refrigerator," he means exactly that. Otherwise the guest may starve, while the host may remain blissfully unaware of this behavior or think the individual is on a strict diet.

Quantities of food and the etiquette of serving it

There is another major difference between the Russian and American style of entertaining. For Russians «изобилие» is a must. Skimping on food for guests, or serving too little, is unthinkable. In America the notion of "hospitality," and the kind of «угощение» offered guests is highly contingent on social and cultural factors. To the great surprise of Russians, generally speaking, the wealthier the American—particularly if he is a WASP (a white Anglo-Saxon Protestant)—the skimpier the table. A buffet dinner may consist of a paper-thin slice of ham, a bowl of steamed rice, a bit of green salad, and a sliver of cake, all served after two hours of drinks and peanuts. Everyone will assure the hostess that this was a perfectly delicious dinner. After all, you have come to socialize, not to stuff yourself. And as the American saying goes, "You can never be too rich or too thin." For Russians, this is an insult to the guests and flies in the face of all Russian notions of hospitality. It is in the homes of Irish, Italian, and Jewish Americans and of people of Eastern European origin that the tables are similar to Russian ones, laden with an overabundance of food and drink.

When an American hostess offers a dish, if a guest says "no, thank you," he should not assume that the hostess will offer it a second time. A "no, thank you" said out of politeness may leave you hungry. In Russia, however, the dish would be repeatedly proffered until it is clear that no one is going to eat another bite. And at an American table usually no one will be insulted if a guest fails to finish everything on the plate.

Conversation at the table

Unlike the custom at Russian gatherings, at most American dinner parties there is no obligation to make toasts, though a short one is sometimes given by the host. There is no tradition of long toasts or of telling «анекдоты» (*jokes*). An excessively lengthy toast will be resented by the guests (while a Russian toast can go on for a good five minutes). Nor is there generally a «тамада» (*"toastmaster" or "MC" / master of ceremonies*).

The same emphasis on brevity holds true for conversation. Failure to "play by these rules" can lead to real misunderstanding and irritation on the part of both the American host and the Russian guests. The host does not usually attempt to entertain guests (развлечь гостей) by telling stories or anecdotes. Nor does he make an excessive effort to make the guests talk. It is up to them to make themselves heard. For Americans, conversation consists of an exchange of short volleys. Attempts to tell a very long story might annoy the other guests or prompt them to interrupt, and a table with six to eight people will most likely have two or three conversations going on simultaneously.

Nor are very serious subjects popular at most dinner parties. Unless the gathering consists of university professors and intellectuals, attempts to go into depth on subjects such as politics or religion will not be well received. Rather, there is a tradition of «светская болтовня»—movies, theater, sports, mutual friends, gossip, family, friends and, of course, food are acceptable subjects for conversation.

In America, talking about food is a national sport. Americans love to talk about food while eating, chattering happily away about what they ate yesterday and what they will eat tomorrow. As one Russian living in America commented, "On Monday, Tuesday and Wednesday they recall what café they went to on Sunday and what they ate there. On Thursday and Friday they talk about what café they will go to over the weekend and what they will eat there."[107] Americans can talk for hours about whether food is organic, healthy, low-calorie, and "free of preservatives," something that could give rise to a good deal of comic misunderstanding, for in English this means «приготовлены без консервантов», while in Russian «презерватив» is a condom. From the American point of view, "Russians in general are not very particular about food and don't pay much attention to whether food is healthy or has a high vitamin content ..."[108]

Special Occasions

The difference in the ways Russians and Americans entertain is clearly illustrated by the lacuna in English for an equivalent for the Russian word «застолье». Americans do not think that at a birthday, wedding, anniversary, or family get-together everyone should sit around one table. Such gatherings are not seen as a "collective undertaking," but rather as a happy meeting of a group of individuals.

Since in America adults do not make nearly the kind of fuss over birthdays that is customary in Russia (aside from marking a major milestone such as a 50th or 75th birthday), a "birthday party" may not necessarily be a very large or formal affair. Russians are often surprised to see that such a gathering may be a small buffet or cocktail party, devoid of toasts except for one *short* one to the «виновник торжества» (*birthday boy/girl*).

At a Restaurant

Language used in restaurants also provides fertile ground for linguistic-cultural misunderstandings. If the waiter reels off at top speed a list of "specials"—dishes served that day that are not on the regular menu—a Russian visitor may be quite hesitant in asking him to repeat them, and may feel uncomfortable about asking the price of those dishes. Yet in the U.S. that is normal restaurant behavior, for otherwise there may be an unpleasant surprise when the check comes.

Additional tips

Below are a few additional linguistic-cultural tips for some common English food-related words, phrases, and behavior that may be unfamiliar to Russians:

1. Since "dieting" (cutting calories and fat to lose weight) is a national American obsession, the labels on nearly all processed foods currently sold in stores show the number of calories, grams of fat, sodium, fiber, carbohydrates, protein, etc. per serving. Any product labeled "lite," "fat-free," "low-calorie" or "cholesterol-free" is considered a good thing. To an American, something "high-calorie" (калорийный) is a bad thing, to be avoided except on rare occasions, since this is tantamount to "fattening." Americans will rattle on about their pet "diet" of the moment, though two weeks later they may be following a completely different one. Though vegetarianism is fairly rare in Russia, quite a few Americans are vegetarians. Americans do not eat bread with every meal the way most Russians do, and children are not brought up with the idea that they should eat their food "with bread."

2. In Russian a "recipe" is «рецепт». In English this word means the instructions for preparing a dish, though it can be used metaphorically—a recipe for a happy marriage, a recipe for disaster. The kind of «рецепт» you get from a doctor to buy medicine is a "prescription" in English, *never* a recipe.

3. The verb «кормить» often cannot be translated literally. «Мать сейчас кормит своего грудного ребенка» translates as "*The mother is feeding her baby.*" But when

talking about an adult—«Мне нужно сейчас домой, надо мужа кормить»—the verb "to feed" cannot be used unless you are literally shoving a fork into your husband's mouth. "I've got to go, I've got to … make my husband dinner / cook dinner for my husband" is the correct rendering of this sentence.

4. Unlike Russia, in a restaurant "water" in the U.S. usually means plain water, also known as "tap water" (from the tap or faucet), since otherwise a customer specifically asks for mineral water, soda water, a soft drink, or a non-alcoholic drink.

5. A «рюмка» is a shot (glass), and it is therefore not advisable to ask for a "glass of vodka." A «бокал» is a wine glass, as opposed to a «стакан», the glass used for water, juice, etc.

6. Names of dairy products can be confusing. Regular milk (full-fat; whole) contains about 4% fat. There is also 1% fat, lowfat (2%), fat-free, and skim milk (обезжиренное молоко). Buttermilk often confuses Russians, for it is not a kind of rich milk but a sort of «кефир». The closest equivalent of «творог» is "farmer cheese" or "pot cheese" if dry, and "cottage cheese" if it is more liquid in texture. "Cream cheese," which does not exist in Russia, resembles «жирный творог» or some kinds of «сырники». American "sour cream" is generally much thicker than Russian «сметана».

7. When a dish in America is described as "hot" this can mean either the temperature, «горячий», as in "hot hors d'oeuvres," or the level of spiciness, «острый», as in "hot sauce" for shrimp, or "hot and spicy" beef ribs.

8. "Salad" in the U.S. usually means a dish with greens and vegetables, less often a composed salad bound with mayonnaise or sour cream, as is the case in Russia.

9. «Сало» (literally, "lard"), which is very popular in Russia, is considered by most Americans to be rather disgusting. It is used only in cooking, and even then rarely, because of the high fat and calorie content.

10. "Cutlets" in English are the equivalent not of «котлеты» but of «набивные котлеты» or «эскалопы». «Котлеты» as such do not exist, except as croquettes, meatballs, or other dishes made with ground meat.

11. In the U.S. cakes and pies are eaten with a fork, not with a spoon as in Russia.

12. «Бисквит» is "sponge cake" in English. "Biscuits" are either little hot rolls or small crackers such as those served with cheese or hors d'oeuvres. «Кексы» is pound cake or fruitcake.

Bon appétit!

8.

English —
A Linguistic Headache
~

Just as Russian can seem unfathomable to American students, English can present a huge linguistic headache for Russians. The field for missteps in both languages is vast, and this chapter will present a subjective and limited choice of the mistakes Russians frequently make and which, in the context of American language and culture, may create an impression far from that intended by the speaker. Many similar errors, in particular regarding the use of cognates, are made by Russian-speaking Americans, with equally negative results.

The English spoken in the U.S. reflects the American tendency to be practical and pragmatic, and avoids long or flowery sentences or sentiments. Where English prefers concrete nouns, Russian opts for abstract verbs. The English speaker uses shorter sentences and makes full stops rather than engaging in long subordinate clauses, and prefers the first and second person singular to the impersonal constructions or all-inclusive "we" that Russian tends to favor.

Polite brevity, however, is not tantamount to the contemporary jargon fashionable in America, particularly among young people. This version of English consists primarily of a series of verbal fillers with virtually no semantic meaning: "Uh, like, so, man, you know what I mean, he like, goes and then I go." Such English is to be avoided at all costs. Older people, too, have been influenced by this speaking style, and have also begun inserting "you know," or "you know what I mean" into every other sentence, the way some Russians nowadays overuse «слова паразиты» such as «знаешь», «понимаешь», «значит», «как бы», and «вроде». For both Russians speaking English and Americans speaking Russian, trying to be excessively colloquial should be avoided. This does not show that the speaker knows the language well; it merely creates the impression that he/she is not a very educated person.

Diminutives

In English diminutives play a vastly smaller linguistic role than they do in Russian, both for proper and for ordinary nouns. [109] While in Russian «Мария» might be known to her friends as «Маша», «Машенька», «Машутка», «Маруся», or «Муся», in English she is just "Mary," a name with no accepted diminutives. Most proper names do not have diminutives, and efforts to create one are rarely successful, for the wealth of Russian suffixes that produce these variations simply do not exist in English. Artificially created forms such as "Marykins," "little Mary," or "baby Mary" sound highly forced and may be taken as insulting or patronizing. In Russian most proper names have a plethora of possible diminutives. One person named Alexander may be known to his family and friends as Sasha, while another may be Alik for life. There is a similarity here with those American names that have short forms (often called "nicknames"). Robert may be Bob, Rob, or Robbie to his friends. In Russian as in English, it is always advisable to check on which one a person uses before jumping in as people sometimes respond negatively if addressed by a form of their name other than the one they habitually use.

The wealth of Russian diminutives for ordinary nouns can also cause problems in English translation. While a dog (собака) may be referred to as "doggie" or a cat as "kitty" (киска), very many diminutives—i.e. "horsey" for "horse"—are mostly used by small children or by people talking about their pets. "The dear little one" sounds odd, and a phrase such as "the dear little boy" may be used sarcastically rather than affectionately by an English speaker—e.g., "Yesterday we left the dear little boy alone—and he broke our best china." Attempts to translate literally diminutives such as «чашечка», «ложечка», or «ребёночек» will evoke some funny looks from English speakers. Americans do not talk about "our little house" or "a little cup of coffee."

Literal translations into English of many Russian endearments and their diminutives such as «милая», «дорогуля», «ласточка», «солнышко», or «лапочка» simply do not work. A well-intentioned Russian trying to use these may not evoke the desired reaction from the American he is trying to compliment or to whom he is trying to be particularly nice and kind. At best, they will sound silly, and at worst offensive. Moreover, since political correctness and feminism have won the day in the U.S., aside from intimate situations, addressing women in such ways may evoke a highly negative reaction, and surprise from the American. As one Russian commentator noted, «Американские феминистки … если кто смеет обратиться к ним с ласковыми словами: милочка, лапочка и т.д.—пишут в газетах возмущенные письма … В пособии, например, учат девушку, если какая-нибудь сволочь посмела тебя назвать «милочкой», четко и сердито отвечай: «я не милочка, а человек, профессионал … не хуже тебя».[110]

Sexual intimacy

The language of sexual intimacy, with words such as "sweetheart" and "darling," also differs. In bed Americans are inveterate chatterboxes, engaging in a combined stream of endearments, running commentary, instructions, and questions to the partner regarding his/her preferences, while Russians tend to opt for considerably less verbal communication. The question, "Did you come?" in Russian translates as «Тебе было хорошо?» Here "to come" corresponds to the Russian verb «кончать». But a lover who translates this literally in English, and who asks, "Did you finish?" can expect a slap in the face, since to the lovelorn American this means, "Are we finally through with these unpleasant activities?"

Proverbs & Sayings

Americans are not prone to the frequent use of proverbs or sayings. Occasionally, someone will say "Look before you leap" (Семь раз отмерь), or "a chip off the old block" (Яблоко от яблони недалеко падает), but educated people mostly tend to avoid these. Americans often fail to understand literal translations of Russian proverbs. «Купить кота в мешке» corresponds to the English idiom "To buy a pig in a poke," but talk about "cats and bags" will get you nowhere.

Nor do Americans make much use of expressions derived from common superstitions. People do not hesitate to shake hands across a threshold (a sign of bad luck for Russians which is always avoided) and do not understand «плюнуть через левое плечо», «типун тебе на язык», or «ни пуха ни пера». (An English equivalent of the latter, "break a leg," now sounds rather quaint.)

Syntax

Differences between Russian and English syntax can also lead to misunderstandings. In Russian, new information tends to come at the end of a sentence: «В комнату вошел молодой человек». In English the «тема-рема» order is reversed: "A young man came into the room." An ordinary English sentence begins with new information: "Mr. Johnson, the new vice-president of our company, will now say a few words to all of you. " In Russian the syntax is reversed: «А сейчас несколько слов вам скажет новый вице-президент нашей компании г-н Джонсон.» The fairly standard Russian «тема-рема» sentence: "And this person, who was _____ (e.g. a genius, a journalist), who _____(e.g. did great things, traveled to Africa,) this writer who wrote_____ (e.g. the greatest work of our century), that is, Petr Ivanov," is extremely irritating to Americans. An English speaker will tell you that, "Petr Ivanov is a well-known Russian journalist, who went to Africa years ago, and wrote 'My Impressions of Africa.'" Americans react to this kind of syntactic reversal, in which new information is stashed away at the end of the sentence, as a cheap rhetorical device. Such "withholding of information" is used in proclaiming the winner on TV programs such as beauty contests: "And now, at last, here with us in Atlantic City—the new Miss America—here she is—the beautiful, the talented—the lovely—Miss Nebraska!"

Intonation

Differences between the intonation patterns of the two languages often cause misunderstandings. American patterns are extremely "restrained" compared to Russian. When reproduced in English, the sharply rising pitch of a Russian interrogative intonation in a question or interrogative statement, such as «Это *ваша* ручка?»— "Is this *your* pen?"—sounds as though the speaker is annoyed or questioning the veracity of an assertion, when the intention is to ask a legitimate and neutral question. While English does put stress on the word emphasized, there is no sharp intonational rise. The English rendering of questions intended as suggestions, which do not contain an interrogative word such as «Пойдем в кино?» require a modal verb but should not be voiced with a sharp rise, e.g., "We're *going* to the *movies*?" With the wrong intonation, this sentence sounds like either an order or an expression of great surprise—how come, we're going to the movies? We have to study! A more idiomatic way of putting a question which avoids the problem of intonation is "Shall/should we go to the movies?" or "Would you like to go to the movies? "

Incorrect intonation has led to the complaints of many spouses in Russian-American marriages that the Russian husband or wife was "giving orders" or dictating what they should do. Depending on the rise and fall of the voice, "We'll invite them for next Friday evening," can sound either like a question or a declarative statement.

An English statement made with lightly rising intonation and emphasis on the final word or words implies that the speaker is unsure of what has been said, and is asking for confirmation. "Your name's *John*" with rising intonation on "John" is a question, not a declarative statement, communicating the question, "Is your name John? " Or "Bloomberg was elected mayor of *New York*," with rising intonation, indicates that the speaker is asking for confirmation of something he finds surprising. A rise in intonation at the end of an English sentence can also indicate an affirmation or confirmation of a statement. "We're moving the office to the *fourth floor*" or "he got the job of *vice-president*" may be assertions or questions, depending on the speaker.

A Russian question asked in reply to a statement may need both syntactic restructuring in English and a clarification of the meaning of the Russian prefix. Take the following sentences: «Маша заболела.» — «Почему заболела?» «А простудилась». Translating «Почему» as "*Why*" does not work. Rather, the exchange could be rendered as:

> "*Masha's sick.*" "*Oh yes? … What's the matter? / What happened to her?*" … "*She's got a cold. / She caught a cold.*"

Or:

> «Маша заболела». — «Почему заболела? Я вчера ее видела совсем здоровой».[111]
> "*Masha's sick. / Masha got sick.*" … "*How come? That's strange—I saw her yesterday and she was perfectly all right.*"

Literal translation mistakes

In literal translation, a series of common Russian words and phrases reinforces American stereotypes of Russians as rude or just plain odd. For example:

1. Verbs of motion
a) Он сейчас *подойдет*.
"He's coming" or "He'll be here in a few minutes." As is the case with so many other verbs, the force of the prefix cannot be literally translated into English. "He'll come by" sounds extremely casual, as though the person intends to drop in for only a few minutes.

b) Сможешь меня *подбросить* (до универмага)?
If there is no indication of the place where the person is to be left off, this can be rendered as "Could you give me a lift/ride?" or "Could I go with you?" If the place is mentioned—«до универмага»—then, "Could you let/drop me off at …" or "Could you take me as far as …" will translate the sense of «подбросить».

c) заскочить, забежать, сбегать.

No attempt should be made to translate the "speed" implied in these verbs. «Она *заскочит/забежит* к вам после работы» does not mean that someone will literally be "running." "She'll come by/over" after work will do. One American was amazed to hear an elderly Russian woman, who was walking very slowly with a cane, suddenly say, «Я *сбегаю* за хлебом,» (literally, *I'll run to get bread*). "I'll (just) go get some bread" would be a normal rendering of this sentence.

2. Занять/одолжить

While in Russian the verb «одолжить» can mean both "to borrow" and "to lend," in English these two verbs are not interchangeable. Take the Russian sentence «Я *одолжила* Анне 200 долларов».

> *Wrong:* I borrowed (from) Anna 200 dollars.
> *Right:*   I lent Anna 200 dollars.

Or the Russian sentence «Я *занял (одолжил)* у Анны 200 долларов».

> *Wrong:* I lent Anna 200 dollars.
> *Right:*   I borrowed 200 dollars from Anna.

3. Собираться, сборы

«Я сегодня к Вам не зайду. Мы через пару дней уезжаем. Буду *собираться*.»

Of course, Americans pack their suitcases before traveling. But the concept of «собираться» and «сборы» as time-consuming processes does not exist. To say that because we «собираемся» we cannot do this or that for several days would be considered somewhat odd. "I'm very busy, I'm leaving soon and I have a lot of things to do" might work. But in packing—as in carrying out so many other activities—Americans tend to act very quickly.

4. Отдохнуть/отдых, праздник

The choice of the standard dictionary definition "rest" as the "one and only" translation of this verb has led to dozens of awkward English sentences and misunderstandings, and to repeated problems for Russians in conveying this concept in their native language. In many situations the most popular and most common rendering "rest" is actually one of the least idiomatic translations of this word, resulting in ungrammatical sentences and confusion regarding what precisely the speaker means by "rest."

Туда не поеду, там *отдых* плохой.
I'm not going there—it's a bad place for a vacation.
(The word "rest" has no place in this sentence.)

Эту неделю я страшно много работала,
сегодня хочу *отдохнуть*.
*I've had an awful lot of work all week, and today
… I want to relax / I want to take it easy / I need
to rest.* (not: "*to have a rest*")

Ну конечно, *отдыхай*.
Wrong: *Of course, have/take a rest.*
Right: *Sure, take it easy. / Sure, relax.*

Вчера мы прекрасно *отдохнули*—ходили на
такую прекрасную пьесу.
Wrong: *Yesterday we had a wonderful rest—we
went to such a great play.*

Right: *We had a great time yesterday—we saw a
really great play.*

В субботу мы *отдохнем*—пойдем на день
рождения к моей сестре.
Wrong: *On Saturday we will have a rest—we are
going for a birthday to my sister.*

Right: *We'll have fun / We'll have a good time …*
on Saturday—we're going to my sister's
house for a birthday party.

(Note: Here we encounter another problem. In Russian
«сестра» can mean both a sister and a female cousin,
while in English "sister" means only «родная сестра»,
and "brother" only «родной брат». If the individual is
a «двоюродная сестра», proper English is "we're going
to my cousin's birthday party." Conversational English
does not make the distinction between «двоюродный»,
«троюродный», and other degrees of the relationships
of cousins, e.g. second or third cousins.)

Прошлым летом он прекрасно *отдохнул*—
поехал в Париж и на юг Франции.

Wrong: *Last summer he had a wonderful rest*
—he went to Paris and to the south of
France.

Right: *Last summer he had a great/wonderful*
vacation—he went to Paris and to the
south of France.

Russian verbs are often translated as nouns: "We had
fun / We had a great time" are good translations here for
the verb «отдохнуть».

Closely related to «отдых» is «праздник». Consistently translating this word as "holiday" does not
work, as "holiday" in American English means a day
such as Thanksgiving, the Fourth of July (American
Independence Day), Christmas, or Easter. American
English does not use "holiday" in the sense of a vacation
(though British English does).Where an Englishman
would say "We went to Italy on holiday," an American
would say, "We went to Italy on vacation."

The metaphorical use of «праздник» also leads to
incorrect English phrasing:

Ваня такой нам устроил *праздник*! Пригласил
таких интересных людей. Жена испекла
дивный торт! Так хорошо посидели!

Wrong: *Vanya organized such a holiday for us!*

Right: *We had such a wonderful time at Vanya's
place. / Vanya entertained us magnificently.*

And «Так хорошо посидели!» has nothing to do with
"sitting," but rather, "We really enjoyed ourselves. / We all
had a fabulous time."

Вчера у нас был *праздник*—день рождения
дедушки.

Wrong: *Yesterday at our house we had a holiday,
grandfather's birthday.*

Right: *Yesterday we celebrated grandfather's
birthday at our place.*

5. Встречать/встретить

In English, aside from idiomatic usage such as "to meet
(a) deadline/challenge/needs/demands/conditions/con-
cerns/standards/criteria," the verb "to meet" is generally
used when referring to people, not concepts or inanimate
objects. Since the Russian verb «встречать/встретить»
is often used with inanimate, concrete nouns, literal
translation needs to be avoided:

Мне *встретился* незнакомый глагол.
I ran into / I found / I saw ... a (new) verb / a
verb I didn't know / a verb new to me.

В прошлом году мы *встретили* Новый год в
Бостоне.

Wrong: *Last year we met the New Year in Boston.*

Right: *Last year we celebrated New Year's eve
in Boston. / Last year we were in Boston
for New Year's (New Year's eve).*

6. The verb "to stay"
The verb "to stay" implies a fairly short period of time. In English it cannot be used to mean one has lived in a place over months or years:

У Пети прекрасная квартира. Мы поехали на выходные в Бостон и *остановились* у него.
We stayed with him / We stayed at his place …
when we were in Boston over the weekend.

Я в Америке *(живу)* уже пятнадцать лет.
Wrong: *I have already been staying in America for fifteen years.*
Right: *I've been living in America for fifteen years. / It's now fifteen years since I came to America.*

7. Infinitive and Present Participal Constructions
There is often confusion in English between infinitive and present participial (gerundive) constructions:

Мне надоело *говорить* Вам все время одно и то же.
Wrong: *I am tired* to say *to you all the time the same.*
Right: *I am tired* of saying *the same thing to you all the time.*

У Иры сейчас целый ряд проблем—как *найти* хорошую школу для ребенка, как *устроиться* на работу …
Wrong: *Ira now has many problems, the problem* to find *a good school for the child, the problem* to get *work …*
Right: *Ira has a lot of problems right now—the problem* of finding *a good school for her child,* of getting *a job …*

8. Рука/пальцы

As opposed to Russian, in English there are two words for this part of the body: "arm," the part of the limb extending from the shoulder to the wrist, and "hand," the area from the wrist to the end of the fingertips. The English word "fingers" means «пальцы руки».

Нога/пальцы

In English, the word "leg" refers to the limb from the hip down to the ankle, while "foot" covers the ankle, the ball of the foot (ступня), as well as the sole (подошва). The English word "toes" translates «пальцы ног».

9. Мы с Вами … (You and I …)

Russian speakers often make mistakes when rendering this expression into English:

> *Мы с* Ваней пошли в кино.
>
> Wrong (and literal!): *We and Vanya went to the movies.*
>
> Right:　*Vanya and I went to the movies.* (The other party should always precede the first person pronoun.)

In a list of people including the speaker, the first person pronoun should be the last on the list:

> *Мы с* Фредом и Джоном будем рады Вам помочь.
>
> Wrong:　*We, Fred and John will be glad to help you.*
>
> Wrong:　*I, Fred and John will be glad to help you.*
>
> Right:　*John, Fred and I will be glad to help you.*

10. Extent and quantity

These categories often cause problems for translation into English. Russian speakers frequently misuse the word "some," producing "some" odd constructions in English.

> Зайдем домой к друзьям, у них поедим, попьем (а то я устала).
>
> Wrong: *At their house/place we'll have some foods and some drinks.*
>
> Right: *At their house/place we'll have something to eat and drink.*

> Он кем-то работает в колледже.
>
> Wrong: *He has some job with the college.*
>
> Right: *He has some kind of a job at the college.*

Всё (*all, whole, entire*).

> Всё утро я работал.
>
> Wrong: *All the morning I was working.*
>
> Right: *I worked all morning.*

> Вся проблема в том, что Петя плохо знает английский.
>
> *The real (whole) problem is that Petya's English is bad/poor.*
>
> Also (and shorter!): *The real problem is Petya's English.*

> Снег идет повсюду, по *всей* стране.
>
> Wrong: *It is snowing in all the country.*
>
> Right: *It is snowing in the whole/entire country.*

A wonderful English translation of a dish on a Russian dinner menu suggests that the diners order "Fish Entirely"—a literal (and probably a machine) translation of «Рыба целиком»—"a whole fish."

11. *Such* and *just*

The tendency of Russian speakers to misuse the word "such" often leads to very un-English constructions:

> Профессор показал, что *таким* способом эта проблема не решается.
>
> Wrong: *The professor proved that in such way it was not possible to solve the problem.*
>
> Right: *The professor showed/demonstrated that the problem could not be solved this way.*

> Профессор нас познакомил с *такими* людьми! По его мнению, они лучшие специалисты в этой области знаний.
>
> Wrong: *The professor introduced us to such people he considers the best experts in this area.*
>
> Right: *The professor introduced us to people he considers as the most qualified experts in this field.*

Russians often overuse the word "just" as a filler or as an automatic translation of «всего», «только что», «лишь», or «даже»:

> Я скажу только несколько слов.
>
> Wrong: *I will just say shortly.*
>
> Right: *I will only say a few words.*

> Он *всего* несколько месяцев изучает французский язык.
>
> Wrong: *He just studies French for a few months.*
>
> Right: *He only began studying French a few months ago. / He has been studying French for only a few months.*

Он *даже* не умел считать по-английски.

Wrong: *He just did not know how to count in English.*

Right: *He did not even know how to count in English.*

Native speakers, too, abuse and misuse this word. One American linguist asked:

But just what is *just* meant to mean? It is supposed to mean "right and fair" or "really" or "appropriate"or "simply," but so often people say, "It's just ... It's just ... I don't know, it's just ... you know."[112]

12. Exclamations and curses

The Russian terms «О Боже!», «Боже мой!», or «О Господи!» have several English equivalents, although these are less commonly used than the Russian exclamations. «Ради Бога!» can be translated as "For heaven's sake," but this sounds rather high-flown. «Ради Бога, не надо/делай этого» can be rendered as "Would you *please* not do that" or "Come on, don't do that!"

«Боже упаси!» is "God forbid!" «Слава Богу/Тебе, Господи!» is often mistranslated into English by Russians as "Thanks God" or "Thanks to God" rather than by the correct rendering, "*Thank God*!"

The Russian «*Ну и Бог с ним*!» does not have a literal equivalent in English. Possible translations include "Well, too bad for him" and "Well, nothing doing."

«Черт» or "the devil" is not much used in today's English. «Иди к черту!» can be rendered as "Go to hell!" though the English is somewhat stronger. «Черт побери!» can be rendered as "The hell with it!" or "Damn!"

Since "the evil eye" (дурной глаз) is not a part of American tradition, there is no commonly accepted colloquial translation for the very common Russian verb «сглазить» (to cast the evil eye on someone). The closest equivalent would be "to jinx something" or "to put a hex on something," but these are rarely used.

All languages have their own specific store of insults. Russian, however, has a much wider range of such words than English, and attempts to translate them literally can lead to some strange constructions. Many nuances expressed by «гадина», «подлец», «холера», «нахал», «паскуда», «подонок», «стерва», and «хам» are lost on English speakers, who tend to be descriptive with their insults: "He's pretty awful," "He's the lowest of the low," "He's a nasty piece of business," "He makes me sick." Or an adjective may be used: "He's disgusting/revolting/vile." Russian attempts at literal translation, e.g. "He's a scoundrel/cad," "He is very crude," "He is base," sound somewhat Dickensian. Russian expressions of opprobrium such as «Он проходимец» also translate badly into American culture. An equivalent might be "He'd sell his grandmother" or "Nothing is sacred to him." «Старый хрен» could be rendered as "nasty old bastard," «разгильдяй» as "lazy slob," and «холуй» as "yes-man" or "bootlicker."

Education

The differences between the American and Russian systems of education are reflected in the language. For one thing, Americans don't have a «конкурс» to get into college. They don't «поступать в институт», they "apply to college." Upon graduation they are awarded a bachelor's degree, «степень бакалавра». The terms for college students are also different:

> Он студент четвертого курса.
> Wrong: *He's a student of the fourth course.*
> Right: *He's a senior.*

For a high-school student (ученик):

> Он в девятом классе.
> Wrong: *He is in the ninth class.*
> Right: *He's in (the) ninth grade.*

Care should be used with the verbs «сдавать» and «сдать экзамены»:

> Он *сдавал* экзамен по биологии три раза, пока не *сдал*.
> He *took* the biology exam three times before he *passed* it.

Наука

1. «Наука» can be a field of study or scholarship, not "science," which in English is used primarily in reference to the natural sciences.

2. «Научный» is often misused. «Научные круги» are "academic," not "scientific" circles. But "Academe/the academy" in English means «научные круги», not «академия».

3. A «научный журнал» is a "scholarly" or "academic" journal, *not* a "scientific" one. In English "scientific" refers either to the natural sciences as opposed to the humanities and social sciences, or to methodology, e.g. "the scientific method" of experimentation.

4. «Его *научный* подход к этому вопросу»—if the person is not conducting a study in the natural sciences, this is his "scholarly/academic approach." Someone's "scholarship" refers to his knowledge of a subject and the depth of the individual's research (this English word also means «стипендия»).

5. «Ученый»—this is a "scholar" in any field, not a "scientist," unless it is specifically indicated that the person is a "social scientist" or a "political scientist."

Patriotism and nationality:
«Родина», «отечество», «у нас»

A word on politically correct "patriotic" terminology. American English does not use the literal equivalents for «отечество» or «отчизна» (*fatherland*) or «родина-мать» (*motherland*). "Homeland" entered popular usage only after the terrorist attacks of September 11, 2001, and is primarily used in reference to "homeland security." Americans generally refer to the U.S. as "my country, " not "my homeland," and not, except in patriotic songs or hymns, as "my native country" or "my native land." Russians referring to their «родина» are speaking about "my/our country." The expression «у нас» does not have a literal equivalent in English. Depending on context, «у нас» can mean "in our country," "in our city," or "in our house." Americans are more likely to say "in *my* country" than "in *our* country." Even to Russians, and particularly for Russians living in America, it is not always clear exactly who «наши» are. The writer Vassily Aksenov pointed out just how confusing this word can be:

> Это иллюстрируется путаницей со словами *наши, ваши, новые* и *старые русские*: «Ты говоришь «наши» про «наших»? Про наших советских или про наших американских? Давай договоримся: их наши—это уже не наши, а наши наши—это наши, о-кей?»[113]

Excessive use of "in my/our country" sounds strange to Americans, and "in Russia" is preferable. A Russian psychiatrist has noted that, for Russians living in the U.S., dividing the world into «они» and «мы» is not a good idea:

> «… Вообще эти разговоры «они» «мы» очень вредны, потому, что они усугубляют чувство отчужденности, что и есть психологическое препятствие в приобщении к английскому языку».[114]

On the other hand, a Russian in America, who is speaking about the U.S., can say "in this country." Though in Russian repeated references to «эта страна» would sound rather strange, in English the phrase is absolutely neutral.

False Friends

Many false cognates (ложные друзья переводчика) are frequently mistranslated. These can cause problems both for an American listening to a Russian speaker, and for an English speaker who automatically reaches for the cognate in Russian. Here is a short list of some such very common "false friends."

Авантюра. Not "adventure." In English this is a risky or shady venture or undertaking.

Адекватный. This popular term does not mean "adequate," but "proper," "appropriate," or "commensurate"—"An appropriate reaction of society to violence" (Адекватная реакция общества на насилие).

Адресный. Nothing to do with "addresses." This means "specific," "focused" or "targeted"—«Адресные санкции» are "targeted sanctions."

Аккуратный. This is not "accurate." The English word "accurate" is closer to the Russian «точный» or «четкий»:

> Он аккуратен в делах
> *He is very reliable. / He is a good worker. / He always comes through.*

> Она аккуратно выполнила эту работу
> *She did this job very well/nicely/properly.*

Активизировать. In English this means "to step up," "speed up," or "accelerate," not to "activate."

Актуальный. In English this word means "relevant/urgent/ pressing/ contemporary," not "actual."

Аргумент. In English, an "argument" often is a «спор» as well as a line of reasoning.

Артист. In English, an "artist" is a painter (художник). If he is a dancer or actor, he is a "performing artist."

Бандит. This is better rendered into English as "thug" or "criminal" than as "bandit," a rather outdated word (e.g. bandits of the Wild West).

Батарея. In English, this is a "radiator." An «аккумулятор» is a "car battery," and a «батарейка» is a regular small battery.

Декада. In English a "decade" means ten *years*, not ten *days*.

Комбинация. This should not be rendered as "combination," as the Russian word implies a specific stratagem, strategy, or system of maneuvers.

Комик. In English, this is a "comedian." The word "comic" is an adjective, meaning «комичный».

Курс. This is not always "course" in English:

> курс нашего правительства *our government's policy*
> курс доллара *the dollar exchange rate*
> студент третьего курса университета *a third-year college student / college junior*

Курьезный. This does not mean "curious," which is «любопытный», but "amusing/odd/intriguing."

Митинг. In English, a "meeting" can also refer to two or a few people getting together. The word does not have the meaning of a Russian «митинг», a "mass meeting" or "public demonstration."

Пафос. This is not "pathos," which in English points to the tragic and/or sentimental aspects of a situation. Rather, «пафос» means "excitement/thrill/inspiration."

Перспективный. Thi is not "perspective" or "prospective," which is a translation of «будущий». In English «перспективный» means something "promising/long-range/long-term."

Претендовать на. *Not* "to pretend to" which is «притворяться». In English, the Russian verb «претендовать на» has the meaning of: "to lay claim to / to have pretensions to / to believe one is entitled to / to aspire to / to think one has something against someone / to have something against someone."

В принципе. These words are used far more often in Russian than in English, and should not be translated as "in principle." Rather, "by and large," "on the whole," "basically," or "theoretically" can be used here.[115] And «Это не принципиально» should not be translated as "a matter of principle." Rather use: "This is not of great/fundamental importance. / This is not the main thing. / This is not crucial."

Профиль. This word does not correspond to the English "profile," which means either a face as seen from the side, or a verbal sketch (as in the title of the late President John Kennedy's book, *Profiles in Courage*.) «Это не по моему профилю» can be rendered as "I don't have the training/skills/ability to do that. / That's not my field of specialization."

Сердечный. As greetings, «сердечный привет» means "best regards," or "best wishes." «Сердечный прием оказанный нам» means "a cordial/warm reception." Care should be taken with the English words "heartfelt" and "openhearted," which Russians sometimes overuse because of the seeming link to «сердечный». "My heartfelt sympathy to your sister on the loss of her husband" is an appropriate use of the word, since "heartfelt" is often used for condolences.

> Он—такой сердечный человек.
> *He's such a warm person.*

Характеристика. Be careful with this one. In English "characteristic" means that which is a typical feature (черта) of something, not a letter of recommendation or reference as in Russian.

Экономный. In English "economical" means frugal/thrifty/ practical/economical, e.g., "An economical way of running the household and of cutting down on expenses is ..."

Экономический means economic, e.g. "economic (*not* "economical"), political, and social problems."

This list keeps expanding as Russian borrows words from English but changes the original meaning, and so a cognate does not automatically entail a synonym!

9.

Nonverbal Language

∿

Not only words, but also silences, body language, and gestures are intrinsic elements of the communication process. The distance people stand from each other, their facial expressions, forms of physical contact such as hugging, kissing, handshakes, and gestures, all these convey significant information and take on very different meanings in various cultures. As Edward Sapir noted, "gesture includes much more than the manipulation of the hands and movable parts of the organism. Intonations of the voice may register attitudes and feelings quite as significantly as the clenched fist, the wave of the hand, the shrugging of the shoulders, or the lifting of the eyebrows. The field of gesture interplays consistently with that of language proper …"[116]

Non-verbal sounds also have different meanings. For an American, an audience whistling at the end of a theater performance is expressing approval, while in many countries this would indicate a negative response.

This area of communication is a particularly fertile field for erroneous interpretation of what the speaker is trying to communicate because body language is rarely questioned, and because the problem is unstated. A person who has not understood a verbal statement feels free to ask, "Could you please repeat that?" or to say, "I'm afraid I didn't quite get what you mean." Yet few will venture to say, "You're standing so close to me I feel uncomfortable," or "Why aren't you smiling?" or "Why are you looking away from me?"[117] Nor will someone say, "Could you please repeat that gesture so that I can analyze it and figure out what it means in my culture?" This is particularly tricky in the "what you see is what you get" culture of the U.S., where a foreigner's nuances and behavioral subtleties may completely escape an American's comprehension.

Take the problem of people's perception of personal space, a field known as proxemics. The accepted distances at which people stand from each other vary greatly from culture to culture. Jealously guarding the concept of "personal space," unless they are intimate friends or very close relatives, Americans tend to stand at least three to six feet from each other. Any encroachment on personal space makes people very nervous, for this either implies aggressive behavior or can be seen as a first step down the slippery slope of sexual harassment.

This problem occurs in many Russian-American marriages. One American wife had to explain to her girlfriends that when her Russian husband moved very close to them during a conversation, he was not making passes or engaging in "sexual harassment." But since he was standing eight inches away from the person he was addressing, much closer than the distance at which Americans feel comfortable, these women felt that he was invading their personal space.[118]

The issue of physical contact during conversation is a highly sensitive one. In an America saturated with "political correctness" and virtual hysteria regarding real or imagined sexual harassment, a friendly pat on the shoulder or kiss on the cheek can lead to a court case. Americans are not part of a "contact culture."[119] At best, they belong to a low-contact culture, while Russians are part of a high-contact culture. America's Puritan origins and the individual's drive to protect personal space discourage the kind of physical contact that is accepted standard behavior in many Mediterranean and Slavic cultures. As one American medical sociologist remarked, "We live in a tactophobic culture, one that is very low-touch compared to many others."[120] Another sociologist arrived at an even more categorical conclusion: "Americans hate to be touched."[121]

At most, Americans will shake hands on meeting someone for the first time, or a man might give another man a friendly pat on the shoulder. Close friends do not shake hands, as that is done primarily during introductions and by business acquaintances. In the U.S. a handshake must be short, but firm and energetic. That applies to both men and women. A firm handshake is part of the ethos of "think positive," and of presenting oneself as an energetic, dynamic person. A weak handshake is considered as a sign of weak character—and that applies equally to men and women. The importance of a firm handshake cannot be overemphasized. For Americans, there is nothing "feminine" or "delicate" about a woman who extends a limp hand. This is known as a "dead fish handshake," and is taken as a sign that this is a woman who shows no initiative or vitality, and who can be quickly written off by her interlocutor as unpromising for future business or personal relations. In Russia, however, an excessively strong female handshake may well be considered excessively masculine.

On meeting and parting Russians, and in particular Russian men, are far more likely than Americans to embrace or kiss. In the U.S., such gestures of affection are generally reserved for very close friends or relatives. Though in Russia touching the person with whom one is conversing is a sign of camaraderie, in the U.S. such physical contact is often considered as aggressive or invasive behavior. And while Russian women occasionally walk arm in arm, this is not done in America.

Americans are very careful not to stare at strangers, thereby preserving everyone's "space" and "privacy." Gazing intensely at strangers or even at friends is strongly frowned on, and staring at individuals who have any kind of obvious physical or mental defect is considered very rude.

In cross-cultural situations, understanding the lack of verbal communication—namely, silence—can be as difficult as coping with differences in linguistic constructions. Take the example of the experience of an American professor who spoke fluent Japanese. On a strike-torn Japanese university campus, following a faculty meeting he had chaired on how to deal with the rebellious students, he was finally sure that agreement had been reached, since all the professors had spoken in favor of the points in the agreement under discussion. "All this may be true," one of his Japanese colleagues remarked, "but you are mistaken. The meeting arrived at the opposite conclusion. You understood all the words correctly, but you did not understand the silences between them."[122]

Americans are used to small silences and breaks in conversation, and often find Russians considerably more verbose. Many Russians, on the other hand, are bothered by the American tendency to fill verbal space with empty chatter. Commenting on silences, the British social historian Peter Burke has noted that, "the meaning of silence varies—like that of other forms of communication ... according to the occasion where silence occurs, according to the person who is silent, and also according to the 'audience.'"[123]

The Russian tendency to excessive verbosity is amplified by the structure of the language, which generally requires more—and longer—words and expressions, often delivered at top speed. When shifting into English, stopping only to take a breath, Russian speakers tend to maintain rapid speech patterns and long sentences, which can prove very frustrating for the American listener. Anyone watching a Russian TV talk show or who has been party to Russian political negotiations has observed this pace, such that an interpreter can barely keep up with a speaker, who in turn can barely keep up with his own speech, or with that of an interlocutor.

The language of gestures is far from universal. A gesture which is perfectly acceptable in one culture can be perceived as a serious insult in another. In general, Russians tend to gesticulate far more than Americans; the Anglo-Saxon tradition of restraint and moderation avoids excessive use of the hands while talking. Many Americans who make frequent use of gestures are of Slavic, Italian, or Latin American origin.

The Russian range of gestures is much wider than the American one. The meaning of some common Russian gestures, however, may not always be clear to the English speaker. Some of the most widely used are shown here.

A "V" sign made by raising the index and third fingers to form the letter "V" for "Victory," indicating that a particular endeavor has been successful.

The thumb and index finger are joined in a circle, with the other three fingers slightly raised above them. This is also a gesture that shows that things are going well, that something is fine/OK. An American might simply say, "That's … fabulous / wonderful / fantastic / out of this world / great."

Wiping the hand across the forehead, palm facing outwards, is a sign of relief that something unpleasant is over (i.e. an exam), or that an unpleasant event (e.g., an unwanted visit) has not occurred.

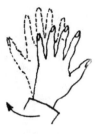

Holding the palm facing one's interlocutor, with fingers spread apart, and waving it sideways back and forth indicates that the speaker has doubts regarding what is being said.

A gesture common to the U.S., Russia, and several other countries is twirling an index finger near the forehead to indicate that someone is slightly crazy.

To count on his fingers, a Russian bends his fingers inward, palm facing him, and the count begins starting from the little finger, usually starting with the left hand. Americans start counting from the thumb to the little finger, counting off the fingers by touching the thumb or index finger of one hand to each extended finger of the other hand.

There are several Russian gestures that can make a strange impression on Americans and are more likely to be misunderstood or misinterpreted:

The gesture of the fist, with the thumb facing upwards, perpendicular to the palm as a sign of approval or praise has no equivalent, and neither does the Russian particle/exclamation voicing approval «Bo!» An American might say—but without a gesture—"That was fabulous/wonderful/fantastic/out of this world/great!"[124]

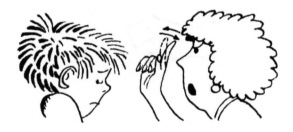

For Americans, one of the most intensely irritating Russian gestures is that of wiggling or waving an index finger in front of a person, a gesture communicating either a warning or a threat: «Я тебе!», «Смотри у меня!», «Вот не надо!» ("I'll give it to you!" / "Watch out!" / "No way!")

Equally upsetting is the similar gesture of waving the index finger from side to side to indicate, «Нет», «Ни в коем случае», «Не разрешаю» ("No" / "No way" / "I won't allow that").

Americans view both these gestures as extremely rude. Shaking the index finger to emphasize, warn, or as a reminder is enormously irritating to Americans, who take this as a sign of a condescending and hectoring attitude. One Russian husband's habit of shaking his index finger at his American wife, as though scolding a naughty child, infuriated her: "Cut that out and stop lecturing me!" she snapped. "I'm not lecturing you," he protested, surprised at her reaction. "I'm just saying be sure to lock the door when you leave."[125]

Pointing the index finger horizontally at an interlocutor's chest, making short up and down chops with it in the air to emphasize a point being made is equally annoying to Americans.

I once heard an American snap, "Get your finger out of my face" as a Russian professor pointed his index finger at him to make a point during a discussion of economic policies in the West and Russia. Such gestures serve to bolster the stereotype of the dogmatic Russian who feels that he always has to be right.

Snapping the fingers against the side of the neck does not mean «Давайте выпьем» (*Let's have a drink*) to an American the way it immediately does to a Russian. Rather, this looks somewhat as though the person is trying to kill a mosquito that has landed on his neck.

Since Americans "think positive," the Russian repertory of self-deprecating gestures meaning «Какой я дурак!» (*What a fool I am!*) often do not come across well. The gestures of repeatedly hitting one's forehead or striking one's neck to indicate «сделал глупость!» (*I've screwed up!*) or «Совсем забыл!» (*I totally forgot about that!*) are prime examples.

However, An American in this situation might put his palm up against his cheek—"Oh dear, I'm afraid I forgot about that."

Other gestures that will not evoke a positive response from Americans are those such as «развести руками» (*throwing up one's hands*), «вознести руки к небу» (*raising the arms to high heaven*), or «опустить руки» (*lowering the hands*) implying that someone cannot do something, has failed, or is giving up—«Что же мне делать?» (*So what am I supposed to do about that?*)—the direct opposite of "solve-the-problem-positive thinking."

Such gestures, which show a negative attitude or reveal failure, run counter to the American approach of "presenting yourself positively," of trying to solve problems calmly and rationally.

Americans often perceive gestures as directed at the interlocutor, not as aimed at oneself or a given situation. Thus an often misunderstood gesture is that of «махнуть рукой» (*to give up on something / to kiss something good-bye / to pull the plug*) with the speaker rapidly lowering his bent arm, elbow pointing forward, at shoulder height.

An American will see these movements not as expressions of despair, frustration, or vexation with the self or a bad situation, but as aimed exclusively at the interlocutor and intended to convey a message of, "go to hell," "get lost," "get out of here." No wonder this one has caused so many misunderstandings!

The gesture of "beating one's breast" in an effort to persuade someone either that the speaker is telling the truth, «Я говорю тебе всю правду! Клянусь тебе!» (*I'm telling you the truth—the whole truth! I swear it!*), or to express some other intention, also looks strange to Americans. The emotion the speaker puts into his voice and gesture can make him seem somewhat hysterical.

The gesture of sliding the hand sideways across the throat (провести рукой по горлу) does not communicate to an American the Russian idea that the speaker "has had enough" (надоело, достал), i.e., is fed up with a situation and does not intend to put up with it any more.

To Americans this gesture is sending a dangerously aggressive message. An incident that took place in a small college town is a striking example of this kind of cultural miscommunication, a misunderstanding that can occur through gestures as well as verbally. A Russian émigré, who was also a college professor of Russian, lived next door to another émigré. The latter was in the habit of taking two large garbage cans out into the street in front of his house early every morning, banging the metal lids and creating a good deal of noise. Though the American woman who lived across the street had protested many times to him that the noise was waking her up, the émigré continued noisily to set out the containers. One day as he was dragging the garbage cans into the street the woman knocked loudly on her window and made an angry face at him. Sweeping his palm sideways across his throat, the émigré gestured back at her. The next thing he knew he was under arrest, for the woman had called the police, charging that he had threatened to kill her, to "slit her throat." The émigré professor of Russian was obliged to testify in court that the Russian meaning of this gesture was, "I'm fed up, I've had it (up to here—up to my throat) with you and your complaints," not "I'm going to slit your throat." For that the appropriate gesture would have consisted in sweeping his thumb across his throat, with the other fingers curled under in a fist.

Communication across languages and cultures is an endlessly fascinating process, filled with potential misunderstandings and pitfalls. Careful observation, study, and analysis of a foreign language and culture, however, can only lead to a deeper understanding both of the foreign language and culture and of one's own.

Endnotes

1. Edward Sapir, "Language Race and Culture," in *Language: An Introduction to the Study of Speech* (San Diego, New York and London: Harcourt Brace & Company, 1921), p. 207.

2. Anna Wierzbicka, *Cross-Cultural Pragmatics: The Semantics of Human Interaction* (Berlin and New York: Mouton de Gruyter, 2003), p. viii. Wierzbicka posits an interesting theory of "primes" or "universals" common to all languages, but recognizes the real difficulties involved in the translation of culture-specific concepts. See Wierzbicka, pp. 20-22, and her comments that "at a time ... when more and more people cross the borders, and not only between countries but also between languages ... and have to live together in modern multi-ethnic and multi-cultural societies, it is increasingly evident that research into differences between cultural norms associated with different languages is essential for peaceful co-existence, mutual tolerance, necessary understanding in the work-place and in other walks of life."

3. The well-known linguist Steven Pinker wrote that, " 'Culture' refers to the process whereby particular kinds of learning contagiously spread from person to person in a community and minds become coordinated into shared patterns." Steven Pinker, *The Language Instinct* (London: Penguin, 1995), p. 57.

4. *Ibid.*, p. 100. The theorists of language as culture-linked can look back to the English philosopher John Locke (1632-1704). Rejecting the notion that words were "the steady workmanship of nature," Locke asserted that they were created by the "customs and manner of life" of a country. [John Locke, *An Essay Concerning Human Understanding,* 1690. Ed. A.C. Fraser (New York: Dover, 1959), vol. 2, pp. 48-49.] And the German scientist Friedrich von Humboldt (1769-1859) argued that while languages had certain universals in common, there were even more concepts and grammatical features that clearly distinguished them from each other, and that many words had no true equivalents in translation into other languages. (For a detailed discussion of this problem see Wierzbicka, *Semantics, Culture and Cognition* (Oxford University Press: New York and Oxford, 1992) pp. 4-6).

5. See Benjamin Lee Whorf, *Language, Thought, and Reality* (Cambridge, Massachusetts: MIT Press, 1998) and Edward Sapir, *An Introduction to the Language of Speech* (San Diego: Harcourt Brace & Company, 1921).

6. Whorf, *Language, Thought, and Reality*, pp. 212-213.

7. Edward Sapir, "The Status of Linguistics as a Science," *Language,* #5 (1929), p. 214.

8. Edward Sapir, quoted in Whorf, *Language, Thought and Reality* (1998), p. 134.

9. Edward Sapir, *An Introduction to the Language of Speech* (San Diego: Harcourt Brace & Company, 1921), p. 219.

10. Edward Sapir, "The Nature of Language," in *Selected Writings in Language, Culture and Personality* (Berkeley: University of California Press, 1949), p. 47.

11. В. Н. Комиссаров, *Современное переводоведение* (Москва: Издательство «ЭТС», 1999), С. 66.

12. See definitions of "house" and "home" in Merriam Webster's Collegiate Dictionary, tenth edition (Springfield, Massachusetts: Merriam-Webster, Incorporated, 1996), pp. 562 and 554.

13. В.Н. Комиссаров, С. 65-66.

14. Edward T. Hall, *The Silent Language* (New York: Doubleday, Anchor Books, 1981), p. 101.

15. For a discussion of such words see Wierzbicka, *Semantics, Culture and Cognition* (New York and Oxford: Oxford University Press, 1992).

16. See Wierzbicka, *Semantics, Culture and Cognition,* and С. Г. Тер-Минасова, *Язык и межкультурная коммуникация* (Москва: Слово ,2000).

17. Dale Pesmen, *Russia and Soul: An Exploration* (Ithaca: Cornell University Press, 2000).

18. As one Russian observer remarked, "The culture of the Western world is primarily a culture of individualists. In Western culture a person in a difficult situation must resolve his own problems. It is not accepted—it's even tactless—to try to dump them on someone else." В. М. Соловьев, *Тайны русской души* (Москва, Русский язык: курсы, 2001), С. 81. —Translation mine (LV).

19. А.Д. Швейцер, *Теория перевода* (Москва, «Наука»,1988), С. 8.

20. In "Letter from Latvia: Language Lessons," *Harvard Magazine*, January-February 2002, pp. 71-73, Elizabeth Gudrais, an American student at Harvard, describes how shocked she was at hearing her relatives in Riga use such popular English expressions. For discussion of the imperative need to avoid these forms in educated speech see William Safire, "Wanna, gonna: Omina leggo of elision," *"On Language,"* New York Times Magazine, 11/16/03, p. 32.

21. Ian Buruma, "The Road to Babel," *New York Review of Books*, 5/31/01, p. 26.

22. Ronald Macaulay, *The Social Art: Language and its Uses* (New York and Oxford: Oxford University Press, 1994), p. 4.

23. Эвел Экономакис, *Какие мы разные!* (Санкт Петербург: «Каро», 2001), p. 9.

24. I am grateful to Pavel Palazhchenko for pointing this out. For a detailed discussion of this word see П. Палажченко, *Мой несистематический словарь: русско-английский/англо-русский* (Москва: Р.Валент, 2002), С. 48-49.

25. Svetlana Boym, *Common Places: Mythologies of Everyday Life in Russia* (Cambridge, Massachusetts: Harvard University Press, 1994), p. 3.

26. Dr. Norman Vincent Peale, *The Power of Positive Thinking* (New York: Simon and Schuster, 1952).

27. See Hanna Rosin, "Happy Days: Barbara Ehrenreich Examines the American Love of Positive Thinking," *New York Times Book Review*, 11/8/09, p. 7.

28. Barbara Ehrenreich, *Bright-Sided: How the Relentless Promotion of Positive Thinking Has Undermined America* (Metropolitan Books/Henry Holt and Company: New York, 2009).

29. Ehrenreich's point of view was described by Patricia Cohen in "Author's Personal Forecast: Not Always Sunny, but Pleasantly Skeptical," *New York Times*, 10/10/09, p. C3.

30. Detailed discussion of the "American smile" is in А. В. Сергеева, *Русские: стереотипы поведения, традиции, ментальность* (Москва: Флинта/Наука, 2008) С. 93-94 and Т. В. Ларина, *Категория вежливости и стиль коммуникации* (Москва: Языки славянских культур, 2009), С. 112-116.

31. А. В. Сергеева, *ibid.*, С. 93.

32. Владимир Жельвис. *Эти странные русские* (Москва: Эгмонт России Лтд., 2002), С. 37.

33. О. Е. Белянко, Л. Б. Трушина. *Русские с первого взгляда* (Москва: Русский язык. Курсы, 2001), С. 73.

34. Стефани Фол, *Эти странные американцы*, Эгмонт России Лтд, Москва: 2001, С. 71.

35. Anna Wierzbicka, *Semantics, Culture and Cognition* (New York and Oxford University Press, 1992), p. 398.

36. See Allan Metcalf, *OK: The Improbable Story of America's Greatest Word* (New York and Oxford: Oxford University Press, 2010), and Beppo Severgnini, *Ciao, America!* (New York: Broadway Books, 2003).

37. See Tatiana Larina, *What Do You Mean? The Pragmatics of Intercultural Action and Communicative Styles* (Moscow: People's Friendship University of Russia, 2010), pp. 11-12.

38. David Katan, *Translating Cultures: An Introduction for Translators, Interpreters and Mediators*, 2nd edition (Manchester, United Kingdom: St. Jerome Publishing, 2004), p. 239.

39. Bernice Kanner, "Americans Lie, or So They Say," *New York Times*, 6/12/96, p. 43.

40. See "Let's Stop the Lying Epidemic," (Editorial), *Glamour*, May 2004, p. 171.

41. An interesting treatment of changes in recent years in American attitudes to honesty and lying can be found in Dan Ariely, *The (Honest) Truth About Dishonesty: How We Lie to Everyone—Especially Ourselves* (New York: HarperCollins, 2012).

42. For the difference between "ложь" and "враньё" see Yale Richmond, *From Nyet to Da: Understanding the Russians* (Yarmouth, Maine: Intercultural Press, 1992), pp. 117-119.

43. Зиновий Зинник. *Эмиграция как литературный прием* (Москва: Новое литературное обозрение, 2011), C. 82.

44. Владимир Жельвис, *Эти странные русские* (Москва: Эгмонт Лтд., 2002), C. 5.

45. Oliver Burkeman, "The Power of Negative Thinking," http://www.nytimes.com/2012/08/05/opinion/sunday/the-positive-power-of-negative-thinking

46. See Lynn Visson, "On Translating Dostoevsky: What is a 'zloi chelovek'? " *Mosty* 1(5), 2(5) 2005.

47. The author is grateful to B. M. Silversteyn for clarification of some of these distinctions.

48. The author is grateful to Slava Paperno of the Department of Slavic Languages, Cornell University for this example.

49. I am grateful to Pavel Palazhchenko for pointing out some of these possibilities.

50. Lynn Visson, *Wedded Strangers: The Challenges of Russian-American Marriages* (New York: Hippocrene Books, 2001).

51. Palazhchenko also suggests "setback" for some contexts, i.e. a diplomatic setback or a football or baseball team suffering its first неудача (*setback*) in a series of games.

52. See Palazhchenko, "The Many Possibilities of the Russian Negative," in *The Washington Post*: "Russia Now," 08/26/2009.

53. Марина Давыдова, «Как перевести на английский "очень неглупый человек"» *Известия*, 5/25/2007, C. 12.

54. David Katan, *Translating Cultures,* Second edition (Manchester, United Kingdom: St. Jerome Publishing, 2004), p. 234.

55. *Ibid.,* 235.

56. Anna Fels, M.D., "A Diagnosis Not Exactly In the Book," *New York Times*, 1/18/02, p. F7.

57. Marsha Ackerman, "Stormy Weather and the Pleasures Of Humility," *New York Times,* 11/8/02, p. A19.

58. *Ibid.,* p. A.19

59. Н.А. Авсеенко: «Особенности реализации категории "индивидуализм" в российских и американских телеиграх и телевикторинах. Проблемы

изучения национальных менталитетов.» В серии *Россия и запад: диалог культур*. Московский государственный университет им. М.В. Ломоносова, 2000, т.1, выпуск 8, С.178.

60. Quoted in Zatsepina and Rodriguez, "American Values Through Russian Eyes," Tesol 99, New York, March 1999.

61. Anna Wierzbicka, *Semantics, Culture, and Cognition* (New York and Oxford: Oxford University, 1992), p. 397.

62. For a detailed discussion of the crucial role of «судьба» and «рок» in Russian see Wierzbicka, pp. 65-116, and Daniel Rancour-Laferriere, *The Slave Soul of Russia* (New York and London: New York University Press, 1995), pp. 69-77.

63. Wierzbicka, p. 105.

64. For a very interesting cross-cultural study of the role of «судьба» see *Понятие судьбы в контексте разных культур*, ред. Н.Д. Арутюнов (Москва: Наука, 1994).

65. «Лучшие анекдоты недели,» www.anekdot.ru, «Итоги», 12/31/02, p. 3.

66. See Wierzbicka, p. 71, and Rancour-Laferriere.

67. These last three examples are from Lina Rozovskaya, "The Discreet Charm of Avos'": "Survival Russian," *Russian Life*, November-December 2004, p. 39

68. See Erving Goffman, *The Presentation of Self in Everyday Life* (New York: Doubleday, Anchor Books, 1959), p. 240.

69. *Ibid.*, p. 244.

70. Erving Goffman, *Interaction Ritual: Essays on Face-to-Face Behavior* (New York, Pantheon Books, 1967), pp. 72-73 and 116.

71. Paul Greenberg, *Leaving Katya* (New York: G. Putnam's Sons, 2002), p. 207.

72. Владимир Жельвис, *Эти странные русские* (Москва: Эгмонт России лтд., 2002), p. 34.

73. William Safire, "I'm Good:" "On Language," *New York Times Sunday Magazine*, 1/8/06, p. 22.

74. Edward T. Hall and Mildred Reed Hall, *Understanding Cultural Differences* (Yarmouth, Maine: Intercultural Press, Inc, 1990), pp. 6-10, 183-184.

75. О.Е. Белянко, Л.Б. Трушина, *Русские с первого взгляда* (Москва: Русский язык, курсы, 2001), p. 25.

76. Quoted in Jan Hoffman, "When Thumbs up Is No Comfort: Treating Illnesses with a Smile and a Metaphor," *New York Times*, "Styles," 6/1/08, p. 1.

77. Lisa Belkin, "The Pandemic of Not Calling in Sick," Job Market (section 10), *New York Times*, 1/5/06, p. 10.

78. Margaret Visser, *The Gift of Thanks: The Roots and Rituals of Gratitude*: New York: Houghton Mifflin Harcourt, 2009), p. 55.

79. Adapted from Ron Scollon and Suzanna Wong Scollon, *Intercultural Communication: A Discourse Approach*. Second Edition. Oxford: Blackwell Publishers Ltd., 2001.

80. *Ibid.*, p. 64.

81. Л. Чорекчян, *Откровения русского психотерапевта на американской земле* (Москва: "КСП+", 2001), p.177.

82. David Katan, *Translating Cultures* (Manchester, United Kingdom: St. Jerome Publishing, 1999), p. 218.

83. Larina, *What Do You Mean?*, p. 12.

84. See William Safire, "I Would Seem," "On Language," *New York Times Magazine*, 9/14/08, p. 16.

85. See Tatiana Larina, "Directness, Imposition and Politeness in Russian," *Cambridge ESOL Research Notes*, issue 3, August 2008, pp. 33-36.

86. See Т.В. Ларина, *Категория вежливости и стиль коммуникации* (Языки славянских литератур: Москва 2009), С. 10-12.

87. Larina, *What Do You Mean*, p. 79.

88. Е.М. Верещагин, В.Г. Костомаров. *В поисках новых путей развития лингвострановедения* (Москва: Государственный институт им.А.С. Пушкина, 1999), С. 18

89. Visser proposes a rather questionable theory regarding the dearth of "thank you's" in today's Russia, suggesting that this is a historical reaction to the huge-scale process of "Thank you, Comrade Stalin" and the carefully orchestrated enormous ritual performances expressing gratitude to the country's leaders (pp. 335-337).

90. "Thank you" can also be said in a sarcastic manner, depending on the context and intonation: e.g. "Well, on this one you can count me out, thank you very much" (Visser, p. 49).

91. Heavy use of the word «неправильное» by Soviet diplomats was a constant irritant, an impediment to reaching agreement, and a never-ending source of amusement for their American counterparts. See Edmund S. Glenn, "Semantic Difficulties in International Communication," in *The Use and Misuse of Language*, ed. S.I. Hayakawa (Greenwich, Connecticut: Fawcett Publications, 1962), p. 48, and S.I. Hayakawa, *Language in Thought and Action* (San Diego: Harcourt, Inc, 1992), pp. 118-119.

92. И.А. Стернин, М.А. Стернина, *Очерк американского коммуникативного поведения* (Воронеж: Истоки, 2001), pp. 75-76.

93. See «Общество», *Известия*, 11/16/02, С. 10.

94. See Katan, *Translating Cultures*, p. 220.

95. Edward T. Hall and Mildred Reeve Hall, *Understanding Cultural Differences: Germans, French and Americans* (Yarmouth: Maine, Intercultural Press, 1989), pp. 13-15.

96. *Ibid.*, pp. 15-16.

97. Geoffrey Nunberg, "Keeping Ahead of the Joneses," in "The Week in Review," *New York Times*, 11/24/02, p. 4.

98. О.Е. Белянко, Л.Б. Трубина, *Русские с первого взгляда* (Москва, Русский язык, 2001), С. 41.

99. The idea of going visiting, «на огонек», is considered by Americans as extremely rude because it shows total disregard for the other person's schedule, activities, and privacy (a word which does not exist in Russian). Not surprisingly, there is no idiomatic English equivalent for this custom, which can be translated as "dropping in on the spur of the moment without calling."

100. An interesting discussion of these concepts of time is contained in Olga Zatsepina and Julio Rodriguez, "American Values Through Russian Eyes," presented at TESOL 99, New York, NY, March, 1999.

101. Белянко и Трубина, *Русские с первого взгляда,* С.19.

102. А.Д. Шмелев, *Русский язык и внеязыковая действительность* (Москва: Языки славянской культуры, 2002), pp. 331-341.

103. See David Katan, *Translating Cultures*, p. 173.

104. Hall and Hall, *Understanding Cultural Differences*, p. 146.

105. Deborah Tannen, *You Just Don't Understand* (New York: Ballantine Books, 1991), p. 207.

106. Barbara Bush, *A Memoir* (New York: St. Martin's Paperbacks, 1994), p. 228.

107. Maria Knjazeva, *America Through the Eyes of a Russian Woman* (Estonia: Ou Mark & Partnerid, 1999), p. 166.

108. В.М. Соловьев, *Тайны русской души* (Москва, Русский язык: курсы, 1999), С. 107. (Translation mine —LV).

109. For an exhaustive discussion of the meaning of Russian diminutives of proper nouns and the meanings of some English diminutives, see Anna Wierzbicka, *Semantics, Culture and Cognition*, pp. 244-276, 407-412.

110. О.У. Белянко, Л.Б. Трушина, *Русские с первого взгляда* (Москва: Русский язык, 2001), С. 75.

111. See Е.А. Брызгунова, *Звуки и интонации русской речи* (Москва: Русский язык, 1977).

112. Roy Blount Jr., *Alphabet Juice* (New York: Sara Crichton Books / Farrar Straus and Giroux, 2008), p. 159.

113. Vasiliy Aksenov, quoted and discussed in V. Kostomarov, *Языковой вкус эпохи* (Санкт-Петербург: Златоуст, 1999), С. 150.

114. Л.Чорекчян, *Откровения русского психотерапевта на американской земле* (Москва КСП+), С. 175.

115. I am grateful to Steven Shabad for these suggestions.

116. Edward Sapir, "Communication," in *Selected Writings in Language, Culture and Personality* (Berkeley, Los Angeles and London: University of California Press, 1985), p. 105.

117. "No one will ever turn to the nice person from Italy or Greece and say, "I like you but you're standing too close to me…"" Quoted in Stephanie Rosenbloom, "In Certain Circles, Two is a Crowd," *New York Times*, "Styles," 11/16/2006, p. 10.

118. See Lynn Visson, *Wedded Strangers: The Challenges of Russian-American Marriages* (New York: Hippocrene Books, 2001), p. 138.

119. See T. Larina, *Категория вежливости и стиль коммуникации: Сопоставление английских и русских лингвокультурных традиций* (Языки славянских культур: Москва, 2009), С. 46-48.

120. Janet Kahn, quoted in Susan C. Roberts, "Contact Support," *AARP*, January and February 2009, p. 46.

121. Dane Archer, quoted in Stephanie Rosenbloom, "In Certain Circles, Two is a Crowd," *New York Times*, "Styles," 11/16/2006, p. 10.

122. See Helmut Morsbuch, "Words Are Not Enough: Reading Through the Lines in Japanese Communication," *Japan Society Newsletter*, XXXVI, No 6 (March, 1989), 3.

123. Peter Burke, *The Art of Conversation* (Ithaca, New York: Cornell University Press, 1993), p. 125. Or, as one English poet put it, "Well-timed silence hath more eloquence than speech." Martin Tupper, quoted in Burke, *op. cit.,* pp. 123-124. Burke quotes the French writer Morvan de Bellegarde as listing no fewer than eight varieties of silence—prudent, artful, complaisant, mocking, witty, stupid, approving and contemptuous (p. 129).

124. For a detailed discussion of Russian gestures, see А.А. Акишина, Х. Кано, Т.А. Акишина, *Жесты и мимика русской речи. Лингвострановедческий словарь* (Москва: Русский язык, 1991), and С.А. Григорьева, Н.В. Григорьев, Г.Е. Крейдлин, *Словарь языка русских жестов* (Языки русской культуры: Wiener slawistischer Almanach. Sonderband 49. Москва-Вена, 2001).

125. See Visson, *Wedded Strangers*, p. 138.